Praise for *The Shareholder Value*

D0440441

"This book threatens to trigger an a [ ] corporations. Written by one of the most respected theorists in corporate governance, it takes aim at the smug 'profit-only' complacency found in business schools and boardrooms. Anyone who reads it will be forced to think—and think again."

—**Thomas Donaldson, Mark O. Winkelman Professor, The Wharton School, University of Pennsylvania**

"The only antidote to prevailing bad theory is calm, careful, plainspoken, and relentless argumentation that peels away the distracting layers of abstract mumbo jumbo to expose the lunacy of the underlying theory for all to see. Lynn Stout does the world a great favor in exposing shareholder value theory for what it is: flawed and damaging theory. Comprehensive yet brief, profound yet enjoyable, this is a must-read for anyone who cares about the future of democratic capitalism."

—**Roger Martin, Dean, Rotman School of Management, University of Toronto, and author of *Fixing the Game***

"It is widely believed that corporations exist solely to maximize profits. It is also widely believed that this corporate purpose is prescribed by law. Lynn Stout shows that these influential beliefs are both wrong and very likely destructive."

—**Ralph Gomory, Research Professor, New York University; President Emeritus, Alfred P. Sloan Foundation; and former Senior Vice President for Science and Technology, IBM Corporation**

"Professor Stout is a leader of a growing group of corporate executives, economists, lawyers, and thoughtful investors who have embraced the concept that corporations should, and indeed must, be managed in the interests of all their constituents. This book is a very readable explanation of the adverse impact that ignoring the interests of all constituents and short-termism have had on not just employees, customers, suppliers, communities, and the economy as a whole but the very shareholders themselves."

—**Martin Lipton, Senior Partner, Wachtell, Lipton, Rosen & Katz**

"Lynn Stout raises a critical question about American capitalism: what is the purpose of the public corporation? For too many years there has been an uncontested assertion that all that matters is creating shareholder wealth. This is an underlying cause of many of the ills facing American society, and this is therefore a critically important book!"

—Jay Lorsch, Louis Kirstein Professor of Human Relations, Harvard Business School, and author of *Back to the Drawing Board* (with Colin B. Carter) and *Pawns or Potentates*

"Lynn Stout presents a thoroughly researched and articulated case against shareholder value exclusivity. It serves the grand purpose of illuminating the debate in the hope of finding a reasoned result."

—Ira Millstein, Director, Columbia Law School and Columbia Business School Program on Global, Economic, and Regulatory Interdependence, and Theodore Nierenberg Adjunct Professor of Corporate Governance, Yale School of Management

"Lynn Stout's engaging book deals a knockout blow to the mantra of 'shareholder value' that has come to dominate corporate boardrooms in the last two decades. While she makes her case in a readable and entertaining way, her message is very serious: the obsession that the business community has with maximizing shareholder value is making US corporations weaker, not stronger."

—Dr. Margaret M. Blair, Professor of Law, Milton R. Underwood Chair in Free Enterprise, Vanderbilt University Law School

"Lynn Stout kicks another brick off of the mantle of short-termism, showing again why choosing to myopically focus on short-term value not only can destroy longer-term performance but also is legally inconsistent with leading corporate governance principles, incentives, and actions that aspire to more sustainable value creation—over the long term and for all stakeholders, including shareholders."

—Dean Krehmeyer, Executive Director, Business Roundtable Institute for Corporate Ethics

THE
SHAREHOLDER
VALUE MYTH

How Putting Shareholders First Harms Investors, Corporations, and the Public

LYNN STOUT

BK

Berrett–Koehler Publishers, Inc.
San Francisco
a BK Business book

Berrett-Koehler Publishers, Inc.

1333 Broadway, Suite 1000

Oakland, CA 94612-1921

Tel: (510) 817-2277   Fax: (510) 817-2278   www.bkconnection.com

Ordering Information

Quantity sales. Special discounts are available on quantity purchases by corporations, associations, and others. For details, contact the "Special Sales Department" at the Berrett-Koehler address above.

Individual sales. Berrett-Koehler publications are available through most bookstores. They can also be ordered directly from Berrett-Koehler:

Tel: (800) 929-2929; Fax: (802) 864-7626; www.bkconnection.com.

Orders for college textbook/course adoption use. Please contact Berrett-Koehler:

Tel: (800) 929-2929; Fax: (802) 864-7626.

Orders by U.S. trade bookstores and wholesalers. Please contact Ingram Publisher Services, Tel: (800) 509-4887; Fax: (800) 838-1149; E-mail: customer.service@ ingrampublisherservices.com; or visit www.ingrampublisherservices.com/Ordering for details about electronic ordering.

Berrett-Koehler and the BK logo are registered trademarks of Berrett-Koehler Publishers, Inc.

Printed in the United States of America

Berrett-Koehler books are printed on long-lasting acid-free paper. When it is available, we choose paper that has been manufactured by environmentally responsible processes. These may include using trees grown in sustainable forests, incorporating recycled paper, minimizing chlorine in bleaching, or recycling the energy produced at the paper mill.

Library of Congress Cataloging-in-Publication Data

Stout, Lynn A., 1957-

    The Shareholder Value Myth : How Putting Shareholders First Harms Investors, Corporations, and the Public / Lynn Stout.

        p. cm.

    Includes bibliographical references and index.

    ISBN 978-1-60509-813-5 (pbk.)

    1. Stockholders. 2. Corporate governance. 3. Corporations—Investor relations. 4. Corporations—Valuation. I. Title.

    HD2744.S76 2012

    658.15'5—dc23

                        2012003687

First Edition

19 18 17 16   10 9 8 7 6 5

Cover design: Nicole Hayward

Project management: Lisa Crowder, Adept Content Solutions, Urbana, IL

Full-service book production: Adept Content Solutions, Urbana, IL

Contents

Preface

Back when I was a law school student in the early 1980s, my professors taught me that shareholders "own" corporations and that the purpose of corporations is to "maximize shareholder value." I was just out of college at the time and not very familiar with the business world, so this made sense enough to me. When I first began lecturing and writing in business law myself, I incorporated the shareholder value thinking that I had been taught into my own teaching and scholarship.

It soon became apparent to me there was a problem with this approach. The more I read business law cases, the more obvious it became that U.S. corporate law does not, in fact, require corporations to maximize either share price or shareholder wealth. My first reaction was puzzlement and frustration. Shareholder value thinking was almost uniformly accepted by experts in law, finance, and management. Why then, I asked myself, wasn't it required by the actual rules of corporate law?

In 1995, I spent some time as a guest scholar at the Brookings Institution in Washington, D.C. While there I was lucky enough to get to know Margaret Blair, an economist also interested in corporations. Blair offered a novel answer to my question: *maybe corporate law was right and the experts were wrong.* Maybe there were good reasons why corporate directors were not required to maximize shareholder value.

That conversation with Blair began my nearly two decades of investigation into the question of corporate purpose. My sense that something was wrong with shareholder value thinking was only heightened when Enron, a firm obsessed with raising its share price and a supposed paragon of "good corporate governance," collapsed in fraud and scandal in 2000.

Writing both alone and with Blair, I published articles on the question of corporate purpose and sought out the work of other academics willing to question the theoretical and empirical validity of "shareholder primacy." Meanwhile, I was becoming involved in the business world myself as an advisor to and a director of profit and nonprofit organizations. I took every opportunity to ask the business executives, corporate lawyers, and individual and institutional investors I dealt with how they thought corporations really worked. The more I listened to their answers, the more I grew to suspect that "maximize shareholder value" is an incoherent and counterproductive business objective.

Put bluntly, conventional shareholder value thinking is a mistake for most firms—and a big mistake at that. Shareholder value thinking causes corporate managers to focus myopically on short-term earnings reports at the expense of long-term performance; discourages investment and innovation; harms employees, customers, and communities; and causes companies to indulge in reckless, sociopathic, and socially irresponsible behaviors. It threatens the welfare of consumers, employees, communities, and investors alike.

This book explains why. It is written to be of use for law and business experts, but it is also written to be understood by executives, investors, and informed laypersons—indeed anyone who wants to understand why corporations do what they do, and how we can help corporations do better.

Although it would be near-impossible for me to thank everyone who generously gave me ideas, suggestions, or support as I wrote this book, I would like to acknowledge the special contributions and inspiration provided by Ralph Gomory and Gail Pesyna at the Sloan Foundation; Judy Samuelson at the Aspen Institute; and Steve Piersanti and the wonderful staff at Berrett-Koehler. This is their book as well.

Lynn Stout
February 2012

"The Dumbest Idea in the World"

The *Deepwater Horizon* was an oil drilling rig, a massive float-ing structure that cost more than a third of a billion dollars to build and measured the length of a football field from bottom to top. On the night of April 20, 2010, the *Deepwater Horizon* was working in the Gulf of Mexico, finishing an exploratory well named Macondo for the corporation BP. Suddenly the rig was rocked by a loud explosion. Within minutes the *Deepwater Horizon* was transformed into a column of fire that burned for nearly two days before collapsing into the depths of the Gulf of Mexico. Meanwhile, the Macondo well began vomit-ing tens of thousands of barrels of oil daily from beneath the sea floor into the Gulf waters. By the time the well was capped in September 2010, the Macondo well blowout was estimated to have caused the largest offshore oil spill in history.[1]

The *Deepwater Horizon* disaster was tragedy on an epic scale, not only for the rig and the eleven people who died on it, but also for the corporation BP. By June of 2010, BP had suspended paying its regular dividends, and BP common stock (trading around $60 before the spill) had plunged to less than $30 per share. The result was a decline in BP's total stock market value amounting to nearly $100 billion. BP's shareholders were not the only ones to suffer. The value of BP bonds tanked as BP's credit rating was cut from a prestigious AA to the near-junk status BBB. Other oil companies working in the Gulf were idled, along with BP, due to a government-imposed moratorium on further deepwater drilling in the Gulf. Business owners and workers in the Gulf fishing and tourism industries struggled to make a living. Finally, the Gulf ecosystem itself suffered enormous damage, the full extent of which remains unknown today.

After months of investigation, the National Commission on the BP *Deepwater Horizon* Oil Spill and Offshore Drilling concluded the Macondo blowout could be traced to multiple decisions by BP employees and contractors to ignore standard safety procedures in the attempt to cut costs. (At the time of the blowout, the Macondo project was more than a month behind schedule and almost $60 million over budget, with each day of delay costing an estimated $1 million.)[2] Nor was this the first time BP had sacrificed safety to save time and money. The Commission concluded, "BP's safety lapses have been chronic."[3]

The Ideology of Shareholder Value

Why would a sophisticated international corporation make such an enormous and costly mistake? In trying to save $1 million a day by skimping on safety procedures at the Macondo well, BP cost its shareholders alone a hundred thousand times more, nearly $100 *billion*. Even if following proper safety procedures had delayed the development of the Macondo well for a full year, BP would have done much better. The gamble was foolish, even from BP's perspective.

This book argues that the *Deepwater Horizon* disaster is only one example of a larger problem that afflicts many public corporations today. That problem might be called shareholder value thinking. According to the doctrine of shareholder value, public corporations "belong" to their shareholders, and they exist for one purpose only, to maximize shareholders' wealth. Shareholder wealth, in turn, is typically measured by share price—meaning share price to-day, not share price next year or next decade.

Shareholder value thinking is endemic in the business world today. Fifty years ago, if you had asked the directors or CEO of a large public company what the company's purpose was, you might have been told the corporation had many purposes: to provide equity investors with solid returns, but also to build great products, to provide decent livelihoods for employees, and to contribute to the community and the nation. Today, you are likely to be told the company has but one purpose, to maximize its shareholders' wealth. This sort of thinking drives directors and executives to run public firms like BP with a relentless focus on raising stock price. In the quest to "unlock shareholder value" they sell key assets, fire loyal employees, and ruthlessly squeeze the workforce that remains; cut back on product support, customer assistance, and research and development; delay replacing outworn, out-moded, and unsafe equipment; shower CEOs with stock op-tions and expensive pay packages to "incentivize" them; drain cash reserves to pay large dividends and repurchase company shares, leveraging firms until they teeter on the brink of in-solvency; and lobby regulators and Congress to change the law so they can chase short-term profits speculating in credit default swaps and other high-risk financial derivatives. They do these things even though many individual directors and executives feel uneasy about such strategies, intuiting that a single-minded focus on share price may not serve the inter-ests of society, the company, or shareholders themselves.

This book examines and challenges the doctrine of share-holder value. It argues that shareholder value ideology is just that—an ideology, not a legal requirement or a practical necessity of modern business life. United States corporate law does not, and never has, required directors of public corporations to maximize either share price or shareholder wealth. To the contrary, as long as boards do not use their power to enrich themselves, the law gives them a wide range of discretion to run public corporations with other goals in mind, including growing the firm, creating quality products, protecting employees, and serving the public interest. Chasing shareholder value is a managerial choice, not a legal requirement.

Nevertheless, by the 1990s, the idea that corporations should serve only shareholder wealth as reflected in stock price came to dominate other theories of corporate purpose. Executives, journalists, and business school professors alike embraced the need to maximize shareholder value with near-religious fervor. Legal scholars argued that corporate managers ought to focus only on maximizing the shareholders' interest in the firm, an approach they somewhat misleadingly called "shareholder primacy." ("Shareholder absolutism" or "shareholder dictatorship" would be more accurate.)

It should be noted that a handful of scholars and activists continued to argue for "stakeholder" visions of corporate purpose that gave corporate managers breathing room to consider the interests of employees, creditors, and customers. A small number of others advocated for "corporate social responsibility" to ensure that public companies indeed served the public interest writ large. But by the turn of the millennium, such alternative views of good corporate governance had been reduced to the status of easily ignored minority reports. Business and policy elites in the United States and much of the rest of the world as well accepted as a truth that should not be questioned that corporations exist to maximize shareholder value.[4]

Time for Some Questions

Today, questions seem called for. It should be apparent to anyone who reads the newspapers that Corporate America's mass embrace of shareholder value thinking has not translated into better corporate or economic performance. The past dozen years have seen a daisy chain of costly corporate disasters, from massive frauds at Enron, HealthSouth, and Worldcom in the early 2000s, to the near-failure and subsequent costly taxpayer bailout of many of our largest financial institutions in 2008, to the BP oil spill in 2010. Stock market returns have been miserable, raising the question of how aging baby boomers who trusted in stocks for their retirement will be able to support themselves in their golden years. The population of publicly held U.S. companies is shrinking rapidly as formerly public companies like Dunkin' Donuts and Toys"R"Us "go private" to escape the pressures of shareholder-primacy thinking, and new enterprises decide not to sell shares to outside investors at all. (Between 1997 and 2008, the number of companies listed on U.S. exchanges declined from 8,823 to only 5,401.)[5] Some experts worry America's public corporations are losing their innovative edge.[6] The National Commission found that an underlying cause of the *Deepwater Horizon* disaster was the fact that the oil and gas industry has cut back significantly on research in recent decades, with the result that "knowledge and experience within the industry may be decreasing."[7]

Even former champions of shareholder primacy are beginning to rethink the wisdom of chasing shareholder value. Iconic CEO Jack Welch, who ran GE with an iron fist from 1981 until his retirement in 2001, was one of the earliest, most vocal, and most influential adopters of the shareholder value mantra. During his first five years at GE's helm, "Neutron Jack" cut the number of GE employees by more than a third. He also eliminated most of GE's basic research programs. But several years after retiring from GE with more than $700 million in estimated personal wealth, Welch observed in a *Financial Times* interview about the 2008 financial crisis that "strictly speaking, shareholder value is the dumbest idea in the world."[8]

It's time to reexamine the wisdom of shareholder value thinking. In particular, it's time to consider how the endless quest to raise share price hurts not only non-shareholder stakeholders and society but also—and especially—*shareholders themselves.*

Revisiting the Idea of "Shareholder Value"

Although shareholder-primacy ideology still dominates business and academic circles today, for as long as there have been public corporations there have been those who argue they should serve the public interest, not shareholders' alone. I am highly sympathetic to this view. I also believe, however, that one does not need to embrace either a stakeholder-oriented model of the firm, or a form of corporate social responsibility theory, to conclude that shareholder value thinking is destructive. The gap between shareholder-primacy ideology as it is practiced today, and stakeholders' and the public interest, is not only vast but much wider than it either must or should be. If we stop to examine the reality of who "the shareholder" really is—not an abstract creature obsessed with the single goal of raising the share price of a single firm today, but real human beings with the capacity to think for the future and to make binding commitments, with a wide range of investments and interests beyond the shares they happen to hold in any single firm, and with consciences that make most of them concerned, at least a bit, about the fates of others, future generations, and the planet—it soon becomes apparent that conventional shareholder primacy harms not only stakeholders and the public, but most shareholders as well. If we really want corporations to serve the interests of the diverse human beings who ultimately own their shares either directly or through institutions like pension and mutual funds, we need to seriously reexamine our ideas about who shareholders are and what they truly value.

This book shows how the project of reexamining shareholder value thinking is already underway. While the notion that managers should seek to maximize share price remains conventional wisdom in many business circles and in the press, corporate theorists increasingly challenge conventional wisdom. New scholarly articles questioning the effects of shareholder-primacy thinking and the wisdom of chasing shareholder value seem to appear daily. Even more important, influential economic and legal experts are proposing alternative theories of the legal structure and economic purpose of public corporations that show how a relentless focus on raising the share price of individual firms may be not only misguided, but harmful to investors.

These new theories promise to advance our understanding of corporate purpose far beyond the old, stale "shareholders-versus-stakeholders" and "shareholders-versus-society" debates. By revealing how a singled-minded focus on share price endangers many shareholders themselves, they also demonstrate how the perceived gap between the interests of shareholders as a class and those of stakeholders and the broader society in fact may be far narrower than commonly understood. In the process, they also offer better, more sophisticated, and more useful understandings of the role of public corporations and of good corporate governance that can help business leaders, lawmakers, and investors alike ensure that public corporations reach their full economic potential.

The Structure of This Book

This book offers a guide to the new thinking on shareholder value and corporate purpose. Part I, *Debunking the Shareholder Value Myth*, discusses the intellectual origins of conventional shareholder-primacy thinking. It shows how the ideology of shareholder value maximization lacks solid grounding in corporate law, corporate economics, or the empirical evidence. Contrary to what many believe, U.S. corporate law does not impose any enforceable legal duty on corporate directors or executives to maximize profits or share price. The philosophical case for shareholder value maximization similarly rests on incorrect factual claims about the economic structure of corporations, including the mistaken claims that shareholders "own" corporations, that they have the only residual claim on the firm's profits, and that they are "principals" who hire and control directors to act as their "agents." Finally, although researchers have searched diligently, there is a remarkable lack of persuasive empirical evidence to demonstrate that either corporations, or economies, that are run according to the principles of shareholder value perform better over time than those that are not. Put simply, shareholder value ideology is based on wishful thinking, not reality. As a theory of corporate purpose, it is poised for intellectual collapse.

Part II, *What Do Shareholders Really Value?*, surveys several promising new alternative theories of the public corporation being offered by today's experts in law, business, and economics. These new theories have two interesting and important elements in common.

First, as noted earlier, most historical challenges to shareholder primacy have focused on the fear that what is good for shareholders might be bad for other corporate stakeholders (customers, employees, creditors) or for the larger society. The new theories, however, focus on the possibility that *shareholder value thinking can harm many shareholders themselves.* Indeed, if we think of shareholders as an interest group that persists over time, shareholder value thinking maybe contrary to shareholders' own collective interests.

Second, the new theories raise this counterintuitive possibility by showing how "the shareholder" is an artificial and highly misleading construct. Most economic interests in stocks are ultimately held by human beings, either directly or indirectly through pension funds and mutual funds. Where "shareholders" are homogeneous, people are diverse. Some plan to own their stock for short periods, and care only about today's stock price. Others expect to hold their shares for decades, and worry about the company's long-term future. Investors buying shares in new ventures want their companies to be able to make commitments that attract the loyalty of customers and employees. Investors who buy shares later may want the company to try to profit from reneging on those commitments. Some investors are highly diversified and worry how the company's actions will affect the value of their other investments and interests. Others are undiversified and unconcerned. Finally, many people are "prosocial," meaning they are willing to sacrifice at least some profits to allow the company to act in an ethical and socially responsible fashion. Others care only about their own material returns.

Once we recognize the reality that different shareholders have different values and interests, it becomes apparent that one of the most important functions that boards of public companies of necessity must perform is to balance between and mediate among different shareholders' competing and conflicting demands. Conventional shareholder value thinking wishfully assumes away this difficult task by assuming away any differences among the various human beings who own a company's stock. In other words, in directing managers to focus only on share price, shareholder value thinking *ignores the reality that different shareholders have different values.* It blithely assumes that the question of corporate purpose must be viewed solely from the perspective of a hypothetical entity that cares only about the stock price of a single company, today. As UCLA law professor Iman Anabtawi has noted, this approach allows shareholder-primacy theorists to characterize shareholders "as having interests that are fundamentally in harmony with one another."[9] But it also reduces investors to their lowest possible common human (or perhaps subhuman) denominator: impatient, opportunistic, self-destructive, and psychopathically indifferent to others' welfare.

This book does not advance a theory of how, exactly, directors should mediate among different shareholders' demands. Nor does it directly address the question of whether some shareholders' interests (say, those of long-term or more-diversified investors) should be given greater weight in the balancing process than other shareholders' interests. These are, of course, critically important questions. But before we can even start to answer them, we must begin by recognizing that conventional shareholder-primacy ideology "solves" the problem of inter-shareholder conflict by simply assuming—without explanation or justification—that the only shareholder whose interests count is the shareholder who is short-sighted, opportunistic, undiversified, and without a conscience. This approach keeps public corporations from doing their best for either their investors or society as a whole.

Why It Matters

It's time to rethink the wisdom of shareholder value. The stakes are high: for most of the twentieth century, public companies drove the U.S. economy, producing innovative products for consumers, attractive employment opportunities for workers, tax revenues for governments, and impressive investment returns for shareholders and other investors. Corporations were the beating heart of a thriving economic system that served both shareholders and America.

But in recent years the corporate sector has stumbled badly. Americans are beginning to lose faith in business. One recent poll found that where in 2002, 80 percent of Americans strongly supported capitalism and the free-enterprise system, by 2010 that number had fallen to only 59 percent.[10] Perhaps understandably, in the wake of each new scandal or disaster, public anger and media attention tend to focus on the sins of individuals: greedy CEOs, inattentive board members, immoral executives. This book argues, however, that many and perhaps most of our corporate problems can be traced not to flawed individuals but to a flawed *idea*—the idea that corporations are managed well when they are managed to maximize share price.

To help corporations do their best for investors and the rest of us as well, we need to abandon the simplistic mantra of "maximize shareholder value," and adopt new and better understandings of the legal structure and economic functions of public companies. It's time to free ourselves from the myth of shareholder value.

PART I

Debunking the Shareholder Value Myth

CHAPTER 1

The Rise of Shareholder Value Thinking

The public corporation as we know it today was born in the late 1800s and did not reach its full maturity until the early twentieth century. Before then, most business corporations were "private" or "closely held" companies whose stock was held by a single shareholder or small group of shareholders. These controlling shareholders kept a tight rein on their private companies and were intimately involved in their business affairs.

By the early 1900s, however, a new type of business entity had begun to cast a growing shadow over the economic landscape. The new, "public" corporation issued stock to thousands or even tens of thousands of investors, each of whom owned only a very small fraction of the company's shares. These many small individual investors, in turn, expected to benefit from the corporation's profit-making potential, but had little interest in becoming engaged in its activities, and even less ability to effectively do so. By the 1920s, American Telephone and Telegraph (AT&T), General Electric (GE), and the Radio Company of America (RCA) were household names. But their shareholders were uninvolved in and largely ignorant of their daily operations. Real control and authority over public companies was now vested in boards of directors, who in turn hired executives to run firms on a day-to-day basis. The publicly held corporation had arrived.[11]

The Great Debate over Corporate Purpose: The Early Years

Of all the controversies surrounding this new economic creature, the most fundamental and enduring has proven the debate over its proper purpose.[12] Should the publicly held corporation serve only the interests of its atomized and ignorant shareholders, and should directors and executives focus only on maximizing those shareholders' wealth through dividends and higher share prices? This perspective, which today is called "shareholder primacy" or the "shareholder-oriented model," may have made sense in the early 1900s to those who viewed public corporations as fundamentally similar to the private companies from which they had evolved. After all, in private companies, the controlling shareholder or shareholder group enjoyed near-absolute power to determine the firm's future. The question of corporate purpose was easy to answer: the firm's purpose was whatever the shareholders wanted it to be, and when in doubt, it was assumed the shareholders wanted as much money as possible.

But other observers in the first half of the twentieth century thought differently about the public corporation. To them, these new economic entities seemed strikingly dissimilar, in both structure and function, from the privately held firms that preceded them. The "separation of ownership from control" that allowed the creation of enormous enterprises like AT&T and GE worked a change that was qualitative, not just quantitative. Public corporations seemed to have a broader social purpose that went beyond making money for their shareholders. Properly managed, they also served the interests of stakeholders like customers and employees, and even the society as a whole.

Thus began the Great Debate over the purpose of the public corporation (as it has been dubbed by three influential judges specializing in corporate law).[13] The Great Debate was joined in full as early as 1932, when the *Harvard Law Review* published a high-profile dispute between two leading experts in corporate law, Adolph Berle of Columbia and Harvard law professor Merrick Dodd. Berle was the coauthor of a famous study of public corporations entitled *The Modern Corporation and Private Property*.[14] He took the side of shareholder primacy, arguing that "all powers granted to a corporation or to the management of the corporation . . . [are] at all times exercisable only for the ratable benefit of the shareholders."[15] Professor Dodd disagreed. He thought that the proper purpose of a public company went beyond making money for shareholders and included providing secure jobs for employees, quality products for consumers, and contributions to the broader society. "The business corporation," Dodd argued, is "an economic institution which has a social service as well as a profit-making function."[16]

To many people today, Dodd's "managerialist" view of the public corporation as a legal entity created by the state for public benefit and run by professional managers seeking to serve not only shareholders but also "stakeholders" and the public interest, may seem at best quaintly naïve, and at worst a blatant invitation for directors and executives to use corporations to line their own pockets. Yet in the first half of twentieth century, it was the managerialist side of the Great Debate that gained the upper hand. By 1954, Berle himself had abandoned the notion that public corporations should be run according to the principles of shareholder value. "Twenty years ago," Berle wrote, "the writer had a controversy with the late Professor Merrick E. Dodd, of Harvard Law School, the writer holding that corporate powers were powers held in trust for shareholders, while Professor Dodd argued that these powers were held in trust for the entire community.

The argument has been settled (at least for the time being) squarely in favor of Professor Dodd's contention."[17]

The Rise of Shareholder Primacy

But only a few decades after Berle's surrender to managerialism, shareholder-primacy thinking began to resurface in the halls of academia. The process began in the 1970s with the rise of the so-called Chicago School of free-market economists. Prominent members of the School began to argue that economic analysis could reveal the proper goal of corporate governance quite clearly, and that goal was to make shareholders as wealthy as possible. One of the earliest and most influential examples of this type of argument was an essay Nobel-prize winning economist Milton Friedman published in 1970 in the *New York Times* Sunday magazine, in which Friedman argued that because shareholders "own" the corporation, the only "social responsibility of business is to increase its profits."[18]

Six years later, economist Michael Jensen and business school dean William Meckling published an even more influential paper in which they described the shareholders in corporations as "principals" who hire corporate directors and executives to act as the shareholders' "agents."[19] This description—which the next two chapters will show completely mischaracterizes the actual legal and economic relationships among shareholders, directors, and executives in public companies—implied that managers should seek to serve only shareholders' interests, not those of customers, employees, or the community. Moreover, true to the economists' creed, Jensen and Meckling assumed that shareholders' interests were purely financial. This meant that corporate managers' only legitimate job was to maximize the wealth of the shareholders (supposedly the firm's only "residual claimants") by every means possible short of violating the law. According to

Jensen and Meckling, corporate managers who pursued any other goal were wayward agents who reduced social wealth by imposing "agency costs."

Why Shareholder Value Ideology Appeals

The Chicago School's approach to understanding corporations proved irresistibly attractive to a number of groups for a number of reasons. To tenure-seeking law professors, the Chicago School's application of economic theory to corporate law lent an attractive patina of scientific rigor to the shareholder side of the longstanding "shareholders versus society" and "shareholders versus stakeholders" disputes. Thus shareholder value thinking quickly became central to the so-called Law and Economics School of legal jurisprudence, which has been described as "the most successful intellectual movement in the law in the last thirty years."[20] Meanwhile, the idea that corporate performance could be simply and easily measured through the single metric of share price invited a generation of economists and business school professors to produce countless statistical studies of the relationship between stock price and variables like board size, capital structure, merger activity, state of incorporation, and so forth, in a grail-like quest to discover the secret of "optimal corporate governance."

Shareholder-primacy rhetoric also appealed to the popular press and the business media. First, it gave their readers a simple, easy-to-understand, sound-bite description of what corporations are and what they are supposed to do. Second and perhaps more important, it offered up an obvious suspect for every headline-grabbing corporate failure and scandal: misbehaving corporate "agents." If a firm ran into trouble, it was because directors and executives were selfishly indulging themselves at the expense of the firm's shareholders. Managers' claims that they were acting to preserve the firm's long-term future, to protect stakeholders like employees and customers, or to run the firm in a socially or environmentally responsible fashion, could be waved away as nothing more than self-serving excuses for self-serving behavior.

Lawmakers, consultants, and would-be reformers also were attracted to the gospel of shareholder value, because it allowed them to suggest obvious solutions to just about every business problem imaginable. The prescription for good corporate governance had three simple ingredients: (1) give boards of directors less power, (2) give shareholders more power, and (3) "incentivize" executives and directors by tying their pay to share price. According to the doctrine of shareholder value, this medicine could be applied to any public corporation, and better performance was sure to follow. This reasoning influenced a number of important developments in corporate law and practice in the 1990s and early 2000s. For example, the Securities Exchange Commission (SEC) changed its shareholder proxy voting rules in 1992 to make it easier for shareholders to work together to challenge incumbent boards; Congress amended the tax code in 1993 to encourage public companies to tie executive pay to objective performance metrics; and, thanks to the protests of shareholder activists, many public corporations in the 1990s and early 2000s abandoned "staggered" board structures that made it difficult for shareholders to remove directors en masse.

Finally, shareholder value thinking came to appeal, through the direct route of self-interest, to the growing ranks of CEOs and other top executives who were being showered, in the name of the shareholders, with options, shares, and bonuses tied to stock performance. In 1984, equity-based compensation accounted for zero percent of the median executive's compensation at S&P 500 firms; by 2001, this figure had risen to 66 percent.[21] Whether or not linking "pay to performance" this way actually increased corporate performance, it unquestionably increased the thickness of executives' wallets. In 1991, just before Congress amended the tax code to encourage stock performance-based pay, the average CEO of a large public company received compensation approximately 140 times that of the average employee. By 2003, the ratio was approximately 500 times.[22] The shareholder-primacy inspired shift to stock-based compensation ensured that, by the close of the twentieth century, managers in U.S. companies had stronger personal incentives to run public corporations according to the ideals of shareholder value thinking than at any prior time in American business history.

Shareholder Primacy Reaches Its Zenith

The end result was that, by the close of the millennium, the Chicago School had pretty much won the Great Debate over corporate purpose. Most scholars, regulators and business leaders accepted without question that shareholder wealth maximization was the only proper goal of corporate governance. Shareholder primacy had become dogma, a belief system that was rarely questioned, seldom explicitly justified, and had become so pervasive that many of its followers could not even recall where or how they had first learned of it. A small minority of dissenters concerned with the welfare of stakeholders like employees and customers, or about corporate social and environmental responsibility, continued to argue valiantly for broader visions of corporate purpose. But they were largely ignored and dismissed as sentimental, anticapitalist leftists whose hearts outweighed their heads. In the words of Professor Jeffrey Gordon of Columbia Law School, "by the end of the 1990s, the triumph of the shareholder value criterion was nearly complete."[23]

The high-water mark for shareholder value thinking was set in 2001, when professors Reinier Kraakman and Henry Hansmann—leading corporate scholars from Harvard and Yale law schools, respectively—published an essay in *The Georgetown Law Journal* entitled "The End of History for Corporate Law."[24] Echoing the title of Francis Fukayama's book about the overwhelming triumph of capitalist democracy over communism, Hansmann and Kraakman described how shareholder value thinking similarly had triumphed over other theories of corporate purpose. "[A]cademic, business, and governmental elites," they wrote, shared a consensus "that ultimate control over the corporation should rest with the shareholder class; the managers of the corporation should be charged with the obligation to manage the corporation in the interests of its shareholders; other corporate constituencies, such as creditors, employees, suppliers, and customers, should have their interests protected by contractual and regulatory means rather than through participation in corporate governance; . . . and the market value of the publicly traded corporation's shares is the principal measure of the shareholders' interests."[25] What's more, Hansmann and Kraakman asserted, this "standard shareholder-oriented model" not only dominated U.S. discussions of corporate purpose, but conversations abroad as well. In their words, "the triumph of the shareholder-oriented model of the corporation is now assured," not only in the United States, but in the rest of the civilized world.[26]

There were at least two ironic aspects to the timing of this prediction. First, it was only a few months after Hansmann and Kraakman published their article that Enron—a poster child for maximizing shareholder value and for "good corporate governance" whose managers and employees were famous for their fixation on raising stock price—collapsed under the weight of bad business decisions and a massive accounting fraud.[27] Second and more subtly, Hansmann and Kraakman's argument was primarily descriptive; they were painting a picture of what had become conventional wisdom about the purpose of the firm. Yet even as Hansmann and Kraakman published their essay, a number of leading scholars and researchers (including Hansmann and Kraakman themselves) had begun to question the empirical and theoretical foundations of conventional wisdom.

At least among experts, shareholder value thinking had reached its zenith and was poised for decline. The first sign was a number of articles that began appearing in legal journals in the late 1990s and early 2000s. These articles, mostly written by lawyers, began pointing out a truth the Chicago School economists seemed to have missed: U.S. corporate law does not, and never has, required public corporations to "maximize shareholder value."

CHAPTER 2

How Shareholder Primacy Gets Corporate Law Wrong

One of the most striking symptoms of how shareholder-primacy thinking has infected modern discussions of corporations is the way it has become routine for journalists, economists, and business observers to claim as undisputed fact that U.S. law legally obligates the directors of corporations to maximize shareholder wealth. Business reporters blithely assert that "the law states that the duty of a business's directors is to maximize profits for shareholders."[28] Similarly, the editor of *Business Ethics* states that "courts continue to insist that maximizing returns to shareholders is the sole aim of the corporation. And directors who fail to do so can be sued."[29]

The widespread perception that corporate directors and executives have a legal duty to maximize shareholder wealth plays a large role in explaining how shareholder value thinking has become so endemic in the business world today. After all, if directors and executives can be held personally liable for failing to maximize shareholder wealth, one can hardly fault them for trying to raise the company's share price by taking on massive debt, laying off employees, or spending less on research and development. Radicals and reformers can debate whether shareholder wealth maximization is good for society as well as shareholders. (Canadian law professor Joel Bakan has argued that the alleged legal imperative to maximize profits makes corporations act like psychopaths.)[30] But making philosophical critiques of the wisdom of American corporate law is well above the pay grade of most directors, executives, and employees in corporations. They reasonably assume that if the law requires them to maximize shareholder value, that's what they should do.

There is one fatal flaw in their reasoning. The notion that corporate law requires directors, executives, and employees to maximize shareholder wealth simply isn't true. There is no solid legal support for the claim that directors and executives in U.S. public corporations have an enforceable legal duty to maximize shareholder wealth. The idea is fable. And it is a fable that can be traced in large part to the oversized effects of a single outdated and widely misunderstood judicial opinion, the Michigan Supreme Court's 1919 decision in *Dodge v. Ford Motor Company*.[31]

Why *Dodge v. Ford* Isn't Good Law on Corporate Purpose

Industrialist icon Henry Ford was the founder and majority shareholder of the Ford Motor Company, which produced the renowned Model T automobile. Horace and John Dodge were minority shareholders of Ford Motor who had started a rival car manufacturing company, the Dodge Brothers Company. The Dodge brothers wanted money to expand their competing business, and they thought their Ford Motor stock should provide it. (Ford Motor had for years paid its shareholders large dividends.) Henry Ford, well aware of the Dodge brothers' plans, thought differently. Even though Ford Motor was awash in cash, Henry Ford began withholding dividends. He claimed, with apparent glee in his own altruism, that the company needed to keep its money in order to offer lower prices to consumers and to pay employees higher wages. The Dodge brothers were not amused; they sued. The Michigan Supreme Court sided with Horace and John Dodge, and ordered Ford Motor to cough up a dividend. (It was not as large a dividend as the Dodge brothers had hoped for, and the court allowed Henry Ford to continue with his plan to expand employment and reduce prices.)[32]

As this description makes clear, *Dodge v. Ford* was not really a case about a public corporation at all. It was a case about the duty a controlling majority shareholder (Henry Ford) owed to minority shareholders (Horace and John Dodge) in what was functionally a closely held company—a different legal animal altogether. (Shareholders in public corporations, unlike the Dodge brothers, have no legal power to demand dividends.) Nevertheless, while ordering Ford Motor to pay the Dodge brothers a dividend, the Michigan Supreme Court went out of its way to dismiss Henry Ford's claims of corporate charity with an offhand remark that is still routinely cited today to support the idea that corporate law requires shareholder primacy: "There should be no confusion . . . a business corporation is organized and carried on primarily for the profit of the stockholders. The powers of the directors are to be employed for that end."[33]

This remark, it is important to emphasize, was what lawyers call "mere dicta"—a tangential observation that the Michigan Supreme Court made in passing, that was unnecessary to reach the court's chosen outcome or "holding." It is holdings that matter in law and that create binding precedent for future cases. Dicta is not precedent, and future courts are free to disregard it. It is also worth noting that the Michigan Supreme Court's remark about the purpose of the corporation was not only dicta but mealy mouthed dicta: note the qualifier "primarily." Nevertheless, nearly a century later, this language from *Dodge v. Ford* is routinely offered as Exhibit A in the case for shareholder value thinking. Indeed, *Dodge v. Ford* is often cited as the only legal authority for the proposition that corporate law requires directors to maximize shareholder value.[34]

This pattern makes any good corporate lawyer deeply suspicious. Law is a bit like wine. A certain amount of aging adds weight and flavor, but after too many years, law tends to go bad. A legal opinion that is nearly a century old is likely to be an undrinkable vintage. Moreover, *Dodge v. Ford* hails from Michigan, which has become something of a backwoods of corporate jurisprudence. For historical reasons, the jurisdiction that really counts today on questions of corporate law is Delaware, where more than half of Fortune 500 companies are incorporated. One of the reasons Delaware has become so popular is that Delaware judges (called "chancellors") are renowned for their expertise on corporate law. And in the past 30 years, the Delaware court has cited *Dodge v. Ford* exactly once—not on the question of corporate purpose, but on the question of controlling shareholders' duties to minority shareholders.[35]

The Real Law on Corporate Purpose

So, *Dodge v. Ford's* description of corporate purpose is mere dicta in an antiquated case that did not involve a public corporation, and that has not been validated by today's Delaware courts. Is there other solid legal authority to support the proposition that the law requires directors of public corporations to maximize shareholder value?

The answer is, no. Corporate law generally can be found in three places: (1) "internal" law (the requirements of a particular corporation's charter and by-laws); (2) state codes and statutes; and (3) state case law. (Federal securities laws require public corporations to disclose information to investors, but the feds mostly take a "hands-off" approach to internal corporate governance, leaving the rules to be set by the states; this division of labor has been reinforced by court decisions slapping down Securities Exchange Commission

(SEC) rules that interfere too directly with state corporate law.)[36] None of the three sources of state corporate law requires shareholder primacy.

Let us begin with internal corporate law. Most states allow or require a company's charter or articles of incorporation—the founding document of every corporation and the equivalent of its constitution—to include an affirmative statement describing and limiting the corporation's purpose.[37] If a company's founders wanted to, they could easily put a provision in the articles stating (to parrot *Dodge v. Ford*) that the company's purpose is "the profit of the stockholders." Such provisions are as rare as unicorns. The overwhelming majority of corporate charters simply state that the corporation's purpose is to do anything "lawful."[38]

State statutes similarly refuse to mandate shareholder primacy. To start with the most important example, Delaware's corporate code does not say anything about corporate purpose other than to reaffirm that corporations "can be formed to conduct or promote any lawful business or purposes."[39] A majority of the remaining state corporate statutes contain provisions that reject shareholder primacy by providing that directors may serve the interests not only of shareholders but of other constituencies as well, such as employees, customers, creditors, and the local community.[40]

Finally, let us turn to the third important source of corporate law, judicial opinions from state courts, like *Dodge v. Ford*. There are many modern cases in which judges have off-handedly remarked, again in dicta, that directors owe duties to shareholders.[41] Most judicial opinions, however, describe directors' duties as being owed "to the corporation and its shareholders."[42] This formulation clearly implies the two are not the same.[43] Moreover, some cases explicitly state that directors can look beyond shareholder wealth in deciding what is best for "the corporation." For example, in the 1985 opinion *Unocal Corp. v. Mesa Petroleum Co.*, the Delaware Supreme

Court stated that in weighing the merits of a business transaction, directors can consider "the impact on 'constituencies'
other than shareholders (i.e., creditors, customers, employees, and perhaps even the community generally)."[44]

As in *Dodge v. Ford* itself, however, such judicial musings
remain mere dicta. If we really want to know what the law
requires when it comes to corporate purpose, we have to look
beyond dicta at holdings—will a court actually hold a board
of directors liable for failing to maximize shareholder wealth?
Here, to use Sherlock Holmes's famous analysis, the important legal clue is the dog that is not barking. Judges may say
different things about what the public corporation's purpose
should be. But they uniformly refuse to actually impose legal
sanctions on directors or executives for failing to pursue one
purpose over another. In particular, courts refuse to hold directors of public corporations legally accountable for failing
to maximize shareholder wealth.

How "The Business Judgment Rule" Rules Out Shareholder Primacy

The reason can be found in an important corporate law doctrine called the "business judgment rule." In brief, the business judgment rule holds that, so long as a board of directors
is not tainted by personal conflicts of interest and makes a
reasonable effort to become informed, courts will not second-
guess the board's decisions about what is best for the company—even when those decisions seem to harm shareholder
value. In one famous case, for example, the corporation that
owned the Chicago Cubs refused to hold night games at
Wrigley Field. Although holding night games would likely
have increased attendance and profits, the president of the
corporation, chewing-gum heir Philip K. Wrigley, believed
that baseball should be a "daytime sport" and that installing

lights would disturb the peace of the surrounding neighbor-
hood. Philip Wrigley also supposedly admitted that he was
not particularly interested in the financial consequences for
the Cubs. Nevertheless, the court ruled that that under the
business judgment rule, it could not disturb the Cubs board's
decision to stick to daytime ball, absent evidence of fraud, il-
legality, or conflict of interest.[45]

An even more important example of how the business
judgment rule gives directors discretion to pursue goals other
than shareholder value can be found in the recent Delaware
case of *Air Products Inc. v. Airgas, Inc.* Airgas' stock had been
trading in the $40s and $50s. Nevertheless, the directors of
Airgas refused the amorous takeover advances of Air Products,
which wanted to purchase Airgas by paying its shareholders
$70 a share. Many of the Airgas' shareholders supported the
sale as an easy opportunity to increase their wealth. But the
Delaware court held that, so long as Airgas' directors wanted
Airgas to remain a public company, the Airgas board was "not
under any per se duty to maximize shareholder value in the
short term, even in the context of a takeover."[46] Disinterested
and informed directors were free to ignore today's stock price
in favor of looking to the "long term"—and also free to decide
what was in "the corporation's" long-term interests.

Indeed, there is only one significant modern case—the
1986 case of *Revlon, Inc. v. MacAndrews & Forbes Holdings,
Inc.*[47]—where a Delaware court has held an unconflicted board
of directors liable for failing to maximize shareholder value.
(In addition to the dusty *Dodge v. Ford*, Revlon is the second
case shareholder primacy advocates typically cite in support of
shareholder wealth maximization.) A closer look at the unique
facts of *Revlon* shows it is the exception that proves the rule. The
directors of Revlon had decided that Revlon, a public corporation, would be sold off to a private group of shareholders, thus
becoming a private company. In other words, Revlon's board
planned to "go private," and require the public shareholders of

Revlon to give up their interests in the company and receive cash or other securities in return for their Revlon shares. That meant there would be no public corporation whose long-term interests the board might consider. The Delaware Supreme Court held that, under the circumstances, the business judgment rule did not apply and Revlon's directors had a duty to get the public shareholders (soon to be ex-shareholders) the best possible price for their shares.

In other words, it is only when a public corporation is about to stop being a public corporation that directors lose the protection of the business judgment rule and must embrace shareholder wealth as their only goal. Subsequent Delaware cases have made clear that, so long as a public corporation intends to stay public, its directors have no Revlon duty to maximize shareholder wealth.[48] This is why the Airgas board, which did not want to take the company private, was able to claim the protection of the business judgment rule and reject Air Products' offer to buy Airgas at a premium that would have substantially increased Airgas shareholders' wealth.

The business judgment rule thus allows directors in public corporations that plan to stay public to enjoy a remarkably wide range of autonomy in deciding what to do with the corporation's earnings and assets. As long as they do not take those assets for themselves, they can give them to charity; spend them on raises and health care for employees; refuse to pay dividends so as to build up a cash cushion that benefits creditors; and pursue low-profit projects that benefit the community, society, or the environment. They can do all these things even if the result is to decrease—not increase— shareholder value.

If Not Shareholder Value, Then What?

It is time to exorcise the ghost of *Dodge v. Ford* from contemporary discussions of corporate purpose. Contrary to the conventional wisdom, American corporate law (case law, statutes, and corporate charters) fiercely protects directors' power to sacrifice shareholder value in the pursuit of other corporate goals. So long as a board can claim its members honestly believe that what they're doing is best for "the corporation in the long run," courts will not interfere with a disinterested board's decisions—even decisions that reduce share price today.

As far as the law is concerned, maximizing shareholder value is not a requirement; it is just one possible corporate objective out of many. Directors and executives can run corporations to maximize shareholder value, but unless the corporate charter provides otherwise, they are free to pursue any other lawful purpose as well. Maximizing shareholder value is not a managerial obligation, it is a managerial choice.

But might it be the best choice? Even if the law doesn't require directors and executives to maximize shareholder value, could pursuing that objective be the best way to serve the interests of shareholders, and possibly society as a whole?

The next chapter looks at the normative case for shareholder value thinking. That is, it looks at the claim that whatever the law may require, maximizing shareholder value remains the best philosophy of corporate management because it ultimately is the best way to maximize corporations' economic contributions to society. As we shall see, there is every reason to believe this belief also is mistaken, for it rests in turn on a fundamentally mistaken idea in economic theory: the "principal-agent" model of the corporation.

CHAPTER 3

How Shareholder Primacy Gets Corporate Economics Wrong

The idea of shareholder primacy has gained enormous traction among laymen, journalists, economists, and business leaders. But as we have just seen, American law does not actually mandate shareholder primacy. Many legal experts acknowledge this misfit.[49] For example, Hansmann and Kraakman recognized the yawning gap between shareholder value ideology and the actual rules of corporate law in their influential "End of History" essay when they suggested that shareholder value thinking would lead to the eventual "reform" of corporate law, implicitly conceding that the law in its current "unreformed" state falls far from the shareholder primacy ideal.[50]

Nevertheless, many legal scholars today passionately embrace shareholder value as a normative goal. They believe that even though the law does not require managers to maximize shareholder wealth, it *ought* to. The perceived superiority of the shareholder-oriented model has inspired a generation of would-be reformers to work tirelessly at thinking up new ways to "improve" corporate governance so that managers will focus more on shareholder value. For example, there is now a small academic cottage industry in churning out proposals for tying directors' and executives' compensation to share

price performance.[51] Another popular argument is that corporations should be forced to abandon anti-takeover defenses
like "staggered boards" and "poison pills," which help directors of firms like Airgas to fend off a hostile takeover bidder
offering a premium price.[52] Yet another idea in fashion is that
public corporations need more "shareholder democracy," and
should be forced to eliminate classified share structures that
give some shareholders superior voting rights, or even give
dissident shareholders access to corporate funds to mount
proxy contests to remove incumbent directors.[53]

Intellectual Origins of Shareholder Primacy: The Principal-Agent Model

Where did the notion that American corporate governance is
defective come from? How did maximizing shareholder value
get elevated to the level of Mom and apple pie as an American
ideal? Shareholder value thinking cannot be explained as a
reaction to recent corporate scandals and disasters, as it dates
back much earlier, at least to Milton Freidman's 1970 ode to
shareholders in the pages of Sunday *New York Times*.[54] The
assumption that corporations should maximize shareholder
wealth was already widespread in economic and legal circles
by the early 1980s, well before Enron and AIG became household names. Rather than being driven by recent business
scandals, the shift to the shareholder-oriented model oc-
curred much earlier, and seems to have been inspired not by
experience or evidence but by the seductive appeal of an *idea:*
the principal-agent model of the corporation.

The principal-agent model of the corporation is associated
with a classic *Journal of Finance* article published in 1976 by
business school dean William Meckling and finance economist Michael Jensen. Ambitiously titled "The Theory of the
Firm," the article described the economic problem that arises

when the owner of a business or "firm" (the principal) hires someone else (the agent) to manage the business on a day-to-day basis. Because the agent/manager does all the work while the owner/principal gets all the profits from the business, a self-interested agent/manager can be expected to shirk, or even steal, at the owner's expense. The result is a separation of ownership from control that creates "agency costs."

Jensen's and Meckling's article, the most frequently cited article in business academia today,[55] assumed without discussion that shareholders in corporations played the role of principal/owner, while "managers" (directors and executives) are the shareholder's agents. Yet Jensen and Meckling were economists, not businessmen or corporate lawyers. We shall soon see how their article failed to capture the real economic structure of public companies with directors, executives, shareholders, debtholders, and other stakeholders. Nevertheless, the principal-agent model was enthusiastically embraced by the emerging Law and Economics school as the perfect way to bring the rigor of economic theory to the messy business of corporate law. As early as 1980, Richard Posner of Chicago Law School and Kenneth Scott of Stanford Law School published and edited a volume called *The Economics of Corporate Law and Securities Regulation* that included Jensen's and Meckling's work.[56] The principle-agent model embedded itself still more deeply into scholarly thought in 1991, when Frank Easterbrook and Daniel Fischel (also both from Chicago Law School) published the *The Economic Structure of Corporate Law*, an influential primer still in use today.[57] By 2001, Hansmann and Kraakman were ready to declare that the standard shareholder-oriented model of the corporation had achieved "ideological hegemony."[58]

Basic Assumptions Underlying the Principal-Agent Approach

The "standard" principal-agent model is associated with three core assumptions about the economic structure of corporations. These are:

1. Shareholders own corporations;

2. Shareholders are the residual claimants in corporations, meaning they receive all profits left over after the company's contractual obligations to its creditors, employees, customers, and suppliers have been satisfied;

3. Shareholders are principals who hire directors and executives to act as their agents.

These three assumptions reveal a basic problem with the standard principal-agent model of the corporation. Put bluntly, *the model is wrong*. Not wrong in an ethical or moral sense: there's nothing objectionable about a principal hiring an agent. But it's patently and demonstrably wrong, as a descriptive matter, to claim that Jensen's and Meckling's simple model captures the economic reality of a public corporation with thousands of shareholders, scores of executives, and a dozen or more directors. The standard model may describe some kinds of "firms," especially sole proprietorships, or closely held corporations with a single shareholder and no debt. But it grossly misstates the economic structure of public corporations. To see why, let's revisit each of the model's core assumptions.

The First Mistaken Assumption: Shareholders Own Corporations

Laypersons and journalists, and even the occasional economist like Milton Friedman, often casually assert that shareholders "own" corporations. Sometimes even law professors—who know better—find themselves reflexively repeating the phrase. But from a legal perspective, shareholders do not, and cannot, own corporations. *Corporations are independent legal entities that own themselves*, just as human beings own themselves.

Adult humans can hold property in their own names, bind themselves to perform contracts, and be held liable for committing torts. Corporations can do all these things, too. Nonlawyers may find it hard to wrap their heads around the notion that an intangible and abstract institution like a corporation is a "juridical person." But law has long been used to create—to make "corporate"—institutions that interact on equal legal footing with natural persons. Examples include not only business corporations, but also nonprofit entities like universities, trusts, towns and municipalities, and the Roman Catholic Church. (Each of these legal entities, it is worth pointing out, manages to function despite lacking shareholders.)

What, then, do shareholders own? The labels "shareholder" and "stockholder" give the answer. Shareholders *own shares of stock*. A share of stock, in turn, is simply a contract between the shareholder and the corporation, a contract that gives the shareholder very limited rights under limited circumstances. (Owning shares in Apple doesn't entitle you to help yourself to the wares in the Apple store.) In this sense stockholders are no different from bondholders, suppliers, and employees. All have contractual relationships with the corporate entity. None "owns" the company itself.

Indeed, once we recognize that corporations and share-holders contract with each other, the "ownership" argument for shareholder primacy disintegrates in the face of economic theory itself. Only three years after Milton Friedman championed the idea of shareholder ownership in the *New York Times,* Nobel-prize winners Fischer Black and Myron Scholes published their famous paper on options pricing, which provides the foundation for modern options theory.[59] Black and Scholes proved that once a corporation issues debt, one can just as correctly say the debtholder has purchased the right to the corporation's future profits from the corporation while also selling a call option (the right to any increase in the company's value above a certain point) to the shareholders, as say the shareholders purchased the right to the corporation's profits from the company but have also bought a put option (the right to avoid any loss in the company's value below a certain point) from the debtholders. In other words, from an options theory perspective, shareholders and debtholders alike have equal—and equally fallacious—claims to corporate "ownership."

How, then, can one describe corporations—especially public corporations that issue debt—as being owned by shareholders? One cannot and should not. Corporations own themselves, and enter contracts with shareholders exactly as they contract with debtholders, employees, and suppliers.

The Second Mistaken Assumption: Shareholders Are the Residual Claimants

A second common idea that has persuaded many experts that shareholder primacy is normatively desirable is the idea that shareholders are the "residual claimants" in corporations. In economics, a residual claimant is the party that is entitled to keep all the residual profits left over after a business has met its basic legal obligations (e.g., paying interest due to creditors, contract wages due to employees, and taxes due to governments). According to shareholder primacy theory, shareholders are the only residual claimants in public corporations. Other stakeholders, like employees, customers, creditors, or suppliers, are entitled to receive from the corporation only the minimum the law and their formal contracts require. Shareholders and only shareholders (or so it is assumed) get everything left over after these legal and contractual obligations have been met.

The belief that shareholders are the residual claimants in corporations leads naturally to the belief that maximizing shareholder wealth will maximize overall social wealth as well. After all, if the interests of other stakeholders in the corporation are fixed and predetermined, the only way to increase the value of the shareholders' residual interest is to increase the value of the corporation itself.[60] Conversely, when the value of the shareholders' interests decreases, this must mean the value of the company has declined.

The idea is elegant, appealing—and wrong. To understand why, it's useful to start by recognizing that the "shareholders are the residual claimants" idea has its roots in bankruptcy law, where courts distributing the assets of liquidated companies are assumed to pay stockholders last, and only after the claims of employees, debtholders, and other creditors have been paid in full. But even in bankruptcies, influential UCLA scholar Lynn LoPucki has shown, courts often require creditors to share in equity holders' losses to some extent.[61] More important, we should not judge the function of a living, profit-generating corporation by the way we treat a company being liquidated in bankruptcy court. Living corporations are different entities with fundamentally different purposes than dead corporations, just as living horses (which we employ as competitive athletes and family pets) have fundamentally different purposes from dead horses (which we use, if at all, for glue and pet food).

If we focus on successful, operating companies, it quickly becomes apparent that as a descriptive matter, the claim that shareholders are corporations' residual claimants is simply incorrect.[62] Outside the bankruptcy context, it is grossly misleading to suggest that shareholders are somehow entitled to—much less actually receive—everything left over after a company's legal obligations have been met. To the contrary, shareholders cannot get any money out of a functioning public corporation unless two conditions are satisfied. First, under the standard rules of corporate law, a company's board of directors only has legal authority to declare dividends to shareholders when the company is doing well enough financially, as measured by whether it has (in accounting terms) sufficient "retained earnings" or "operating profits."[63] Second, no dividends can be paid unless the board decides to actually exercise its authority by declaring a dividend.[64]

It is essential to recognize that neither contingency is met *unless the board of directors wants it to be.* Focusing on the firm's financial health and legal ability to pay dividends, "retained earnings" and "profits" are accounting concepts over which directors have enormous control. Both depend not only on how much money the company brings in (earnings), but also on how much money it spends (expenses). Directors can't always increase earnings, but they can increase expenses. If a company is raking in cash, its directors have the option of allowing accounting profits to increase. They also have the option of raising executives' salaries, starting an on-site childcare center, improving customer service, beefing up retirement benefits, and making corporate charitable contributions. Thus, even when a company is minting money, it is the board that decides how much of the new wealth will show up in the company's financial statements in a form that can be paid to shareholders.

Second, even when a corporation has enough profits or retained earnings to legally pay a dividend, directors are under no obligation to declare one, and often don't. It is standard operating practice for U.S. corporations to pay only small dividends or no dividends to their shareholders, retaining the lion's share of earnings for future projects. If this practice boosts the company's stock price, shareholders enjoy an indirect economic benefit. But the benefit is only indirect, and vulnerable to the board's decisions. If the board decides to run the firm in the interests of customers, employees, or executives—or simply run it into the ground—the earnings will become expenses, and stock price will decline.

This means it's simply incorrect, as a factual matter, to describe the shareholders of a public corporation that is a going concern as the company's residual claimants. Shareholders are only one of several groups that—at the board of directors' discretion—are residual claimants and risk bearers in corporations, in the sense that they gain and lose as the company's health fluctuates. When a corporation does well, its board may indeed declare bigger dividends for shareholders. But the directors may also decide, in addition or instead, to give rank-and-file employees raises and greater job security, to provide executives with a company jet, or to retain the cash so bondholders enjoy increased protection from the risk of corporate insolvency. Conversely, stakeholders suffer along with shareholders when times are bad, as employees face layoffs, managers are told to fly coach, and debtholders find their bonds downgraded. Directors use their control over the firm to reward many groups with larger slices of the corporate pie when the pie is growing, and spread the loss among many when the pie shrinks. The corporation is its own residual claimant, and it is the board of directors that decides what to do with the corporation's residual.

The Third Mistaken Assumption:
Shareholders Are Principals and Directors Are Their Agents

Finally, a third fundamental belief associated with the principal-agent model of the corporation is that shareholders and directors are just that—principals and agents. Again, this premise is wrong.

In law, the word "principal" normally refers to someone who hires another person (an "agent") to serve his interests. Thus the principal exists prior to, and independent of, the hiring of the agent. Yet when a corporation is formed, the first thing that must happen is that the firm's "incorporator" must appoint a board of directors to act on the corporation's behalf. Only after the board exists does the corporation have the power and ability to issue stock and so contract to acquire stockholders.[65] Both the corporation itself and its board of directors (the supposed "agents") must exist prior to, and independent of, the stockholders (the supposed "principals").

Even more significant, a hallmark of agency is that the principal retains the right to control the agent's behavior.[66] Yet one of the most fundamental rules of corporate law is that corporations are controlled by boards of directors, not by shareholders.[67] This does not mean that corporate law does not grant shareholders certain rights that can give them influence over boards. Indeed, shareholders have three—the right to vote, the right to sue, and the right to sell their shares. But all three rights have remarkably little practical value to shareholders seeking to make directors of public companies do their bidding and serve their interests.

Consider first shareholders' voting rights. As a matter of law these are severely limited in scope, primarily to the right to elect and remove directors. Shareholders in public corporations have no right to select the company's CEO; they cannot require the company to pay dividends; they cannot stop directors from squandering revenues on employee health care, charitable contributions, or executive jets; and they cannot vote to sell assets or the company itself (although they can sometimes veto a sale or merger proposed by the board). Voting procedures further limit the shareholder franchise. Delaware law, for example, assumes only directors have authority to call a special shareholders' meeting, and shareholders who wait for the annual meeting to try to elect or remove directors must pay to solicit their own proxies. Perhaps most importantly, shareholder activism is the classic example of a "public good." In a public firm with widely-dispersed share ownership, shareholders' own "rational apathy" raises an often insurmountable obstacle to collective action. In the words of corporate law guru Robert Clark, a cynic could conclude that shareholder voting in a public company is "a mere ceremony designed to give a veneer of legitimacy to managerial power."[68]

What about shareholders' right to sue corporate officers and directors for breach of fiduciary duty if they fail to maximize shareholder wealth? As we saw in Chapter 2, here too, shareholders' rights turn out to be illusory. Executives and directors owe a fiduciary duty of loyalty to the corporation that bars them from using their corporate positions to enrich themselves at the firm's expense. But thanks to the business judgment rule, unconflicted directors remain legally free to pursue almost any other goal. Directors can safely donate corporate funds to charity; reject profitable business strategies that might harm the community; refuse risky projects that benefit shareholders at creditors' expense; fend off hostile takeover bids in order to protect the interests of employees or the community; and refuse to declare dividends even when shareholders demand them.[69] Contrary to the principal-agent model, shareholders in public companies cannot successfully sue directors simply because those directors place other stakeholders' or society's interests above shareholders' own.

Finally, the right to sell shares sometimes can protect a disgruntled individual investor who wants to express her unhappiness with a board by "voting with her feet." But when disappointed shareholders in public companies sell en masse, they drive down share price, making selling a Pyrrhic solution. An important exception to this rule arises in the case of hostile takeovers, where a public company's shareholders may have a collective opportunity to transform the company into a private firm by selling their shares to a single buyer who, because she does not face collective action problems, can remove an uncooperative board cheaply and quickly. During the 1970s and early 1980s, as the Chicago economists' arguments began to gain steam and changes in the banking industry made hostile takeover bids more feasible, it appeared that just such a lively "market for corporate control" might develop. But a series of quick legal reactions soon brought most hostile takeovers to a halt. These include the passage by almost every state of some form of antitakeover statute; the invention of the "poison pill" antitakeover defense by *uber*-corporate lawyer Martin Lipton; and the practical reversal of the Delaware Supreme Court's 1986 *Revlon* ruling (which at first seemed to require boards to maximize shareholder wealth) by cases decided only a few years later.[70] The end result is that the economic and governance structure of public corporations continues to insulate boards of directors from dispersed shareholders' command and control in ways that make it impossible to fit the square peg of the public corporation into the round hole of the "standard" principal-agent model.

So Why Embrace the Principal-Agent Approach?

It thus turns out that, when examined more closely, all three basic assumptions about corporate structure typically associated with shareholder value thinking—the assumptions that the shareholders own the corporation, that they are its residual claimants, and that they are principals who hire directors as their agents—are factually incorrect. This raises the question of why, as Hansmann and Kraakman observed in 2001, we have seen a "rapid convergence on the standard shareholder-oriented model as a *normative* view of corporate structure and governance."[71] If shareholders are not really owners, residual claimants, or principals in corporations, why should we want to run corporations as if they are?

To the extent an answer to this fundamental question is found in the literature on corporate theory, the answer seems to be that shareholder primacy is believed to be desirable because it is thought to offer the best solution to the agency cost problem described by Jensen and Meckling. After all, directors and executives are only human. If given a broad range of discretion to run firms in the interests not only of shareholders but also stakeholders and possibly even society at large, they might be tempted to use their autonomy to serve themselves. As Frank Easterbrook and Daniel Fischel described the argument in 1991, "a manager told to serve two masters (a little for the equity holders, a little for the community) has been freed of both and is answerable to neither."[72] As Mark Roe of Harvard Law School put it more recently, shareholder value maximization may be the best rule of corporate governance because "a stakeholder rule of managerial accountability could leave managers so much discretion that managers could easily pursue their own agenda, one that might maximize neither shareholder, employee, consumer, nor national wealth, but only their own."[73]

In Jensen's and Meckling's terms, director discretion leads to agency costs. And as Jensen and Meckling also argued, agency costs can be reduced when an alert principal exists to measure and monitor the agent's performance. To the current generation of corporate experts and business leaders, it seems obvious that shareholders should be that principal. It also seems obvious that if we focus on shareholder value and especially on share price in measuring corporate performance, it becomes harder for managers to claim that they are doing a good job for the firm, when in fact they are merely doing well for themselves.

But this is all *in theory*. If agency costs are really as large an economic drain on corporations as shareholder primacy advocates assume, and if changing corporate governance rules to make boards more accountable to shareholders and more focused on increasing shareholder wealth is really as effective a solution, we should see evidence of this in the business world. Adopting shareholder value maximization as corporate goal should improve corporate performance.

And it is here that shareholder primacy theory finds itself most vulnerable. We have seen how, as a descriptive matter, shareholder primacy ideology is inconsistent with both corporate law and with the real economic structure of public corporations. Next we shall see how it is inconsistent with the empirical evidence as well.

How Shareholder Primacy Gets the Empirical Evidence Wrong

Chapters 2 and 3 explored how shareholder primacy thinking is neither required by law nor consistent with the real economic structure of public corporations. Nevertheless, the law permits companies to embrace the goal of shareholder value if they elect to do so. A corporation could, for example, mandate shareholder primacy in its charter (although as we have just seen, virtually no public corporation does so).

But as shareholder primacy advocates often point out, there are less-extreme strategies that companies also could adopt to make directors and executives more eager to embrace shareholder value as a goal. For example, a company might encourage its directors to focus more exclusively on shareholder interests by ensuring they are "independent" (that is, not also employed as executives by, or doing business as creditors or suppliers with, the firm). Another strategy that keeps boards attentive to public shareholders' demands is to make sure the company has only one class of equity shares with equal voting rights, not a "dual class" equity structure where there is a second class of shares, typically held by managers or other insiders, with greater voting power. Yet a third way to give shareholders greater influence over boards is to remove "staggered board" provisions that typically allow shareholders to elect only one-third of the members of the board in any given year, thus making it easier for dissident shareholders to try to replace the entire board in a single proxy voting season. Similarly, removing anti-takeover defenses like "poison pills" makes it harder for the board to fend off a hostile takeover bid at a premium price and so also makes directors more attentive to keeping share price high.

If shareholder primacy ideology is correct, companies that come closer to the ideal of the standard shareholder-oriented model by adopting these sorts of internal governance rules and structures should show superior economic performance compared to those that do not, including increased profits, greater growth, and—most importantly and most obviously— higher share prices and returns to investors. This observation raises an exciting possibility. We don't need to rely on theorizing to determine if shareholder value thinking is best. We can test ideology with real data.

Testing the Shareholder Value Thesis: No Clear Results

Many modern finance economists and legal scholars have attempted just this project. Legal and economic journals are full to bursting with papers that examine the statistical relationship between various measures of corporate performance and supposedly "shareholder friendly" elements of corporate governance like director independence, a single share class, or the absence of staggered boards and poison pills. Dozens of empirical studies test the supposed superiority of the shareholder-oriented firm. There remains a notable shortage of reliable results showing that *shareholder primacy actually works better.*

Consider two of the most popular types of empirical tests, cross-sectional analyses that compare the performance of corporations with shareholder friendly governance structures against more manager-oriented companies, and event studies that look at what happens when firms adopt particular share-holder primacy "reforms." In both cases, the basic technique is to test the statistical relationship between some element of internal governance (a staggered board, dual classes of shares with different voting rights) and some measure of corporate performance (typically share price but sometimes other measures like operating income or "Tobin's Q," the ratio between the book value of the company's assets and the value of the company's shares in the eyes of the stock market).

The result of all these empirical tests? Confusion. For example, one recent paper surveyed the results of nearly a dozen empirical studies of what happens when companies have multiple share classes. It concluded that some studies found that dual class structures had no effect on performance, some found a mild negative effect, and some a mild positive effect.[74] Moreover, at least one study found that multiple share classes greatly improved performance—exactly the opposite of what the standard shareholder primacy model would predict.[75]

Similarly, there seems to be no reliable connection between various measures of corporate performance and the percentage of independent directors on a board.[76] Statistical analyses of the effects of poison pill and staggered board antitakeover defenses also have produced mixed results,[77] as have studies of the effects of compensating directors with shares.[78] One study of the performance of U.S. financial institutions during the 2008 credit crisis found that the stock prices of companies that came closer to the shareholder primacy ideal actually did worse.[79]

The lack of empirical support for the supposed superiority of the shareholder-oriented model has not gone unnoticed.[80] Influential corporate scholar Roberta Romano of Yale Law School has denounced some shareholder-oriented governance reforms as "quack corporate governance."[81] In an important survey paper coauthored with Sanjai Bhagat of the University of Colorado and Brian Bolton of Whittemore business school, she concludes that "the empirical literature investigating the effect of individual governance mechanisms on corporate performance has not been able to identify systematically positive effects and is, at best, inconclusive."[82] The U.S. Court of Appeals for the District of Columbia Circuit recently handed down a similarly scathing critique of a Securities Exchange Commission (SEC) decision to impose on public companies a "proxy access" rule that gave certain shareholders seeking to nominate and elect their own candidates to the board the right to use corporate funds to send proxy solicitations to their fellow shareholders. In striking down the rule, the court noted that the evidence on the benefits of proxy access was at best mixed, and failed to support the SEC's conclusion that making it easier for shareholders to nominate board candidates "will result in improved board and company performance and shareholder value."[83]

Fishing with Dynamite: Why Individual Company Performance Isn't the Right Metric

The remarkable lack of a reliable empirical connection between shareholder-oriented governance practices and better corporate performance at the level of the individual corporation, taken on its own, should make us hesitate mightily before assuming that corporate law "reform" will produce better results. But the evidence of a link is even weaker than it appears. This is because most empirical studies focus only on how governance changes influence economic performance at the level of the *individual company*, typically measured over a few days or at most a year or two.[84] These studies may be looking in the wrong place and at the wrong time period. It is not only possible, but probable, that individual corporations can use strategies to "unlock shareholder value" that have the effect of increasing the wealth of certain investors at certain times, while perversely *reducing aggregate shareholder wealth over the long term.*

To understand this counterintuitive idea, imagine what you might find if you did an empirical test of the best method for catching fish. On first inspection, one reasonable approach might be to do a statistical analysis of all the individual fishermen who fish in a particular lake, and compare their techniques with the amount of fish they catch. You might find that fishermen who use worms as bait get more fish than those who use minnows and conclude fishing with worms is more efficient.

But what if some fishermen start using dynamite in the lake and simply gather up all the dead fish that float to the surface after a blast? Your statistical analysis would show that individuals who fish with dynamite catch far more fish than those who use either worms or minnows and also that fishermen who switch from baited hooks to dynamite see an initial dramatic improvement in their fishing "performance." But as many real-world cases illustrate, communities that fish with dynamite typically see long-run declines in the size of the average haul and, eventually, a total collapse of the fish population. Fishing with dynamite is a good strategy for an individual fisherman, for a while. But in the long run, it is very bad for fish and for fishermen collectively. Fishing with dynamite poses the classic conflict between individual greed and group welfare that economists call the "Tragedy of the Commons."

Part II of this book will explore in some detail several different ways in which shareholder value thinking can create an investor Tragedy of the Commons and prove a bad strategy for investors collectively. Meanwhile, let us stop for a moment to consider what the empirical evidence shows about how the business world's embrace of the standard shareholder-oriented model seems to be working out for shareholders as a class, as opposed to the shareholders of individual firms. In

particular, let us look at what has happened to average shareholder returns in recent years as the business world has embraced the standard model; at modern trends in corporations'
apparent interest in acquiring or retaining public investors;
at shareholder behavior in purchasing shares in companies
that are more or less shareholder friendly; and at the relative
success of jurisdictions whose corporate laws come closer to
the shareholder primacy ideal.

Shareholder Value Ideology and Investor Returns

Turning first to the question of average shareholder returns, it
is notable that even though American corporate law still does
not dictate shareholder primacy, as a practical matter today's
public companies pay far more attention to shareholder value
than American firms did two or three decades ago. Although
many individual investors still hold stocks directly, in recent
decades more have chosen to invest indirectly, by owning interests in institutional investors like pension funds and mutual funds. Pension and mutual funds concentrate the funds of
many small investors and so can end up owning large enough
stakes in individual companies to overcome the rational apathy described in Chapter 2 and seek to influence companies'
affairs. Another kind of new institutional investor, the hedge
fund, is even more likely to concentrate its portfolio in a few
holdings, making "rational apathy" even less rational.

Meanwhile, in the name of promoting shareholder democracy, the SEC over the past two decades has adopted several
rules designed to encourage boards to pay greater attention to
shareholder demands. For example, in 1992 the SEC amended its proxy rules to make it easier for institutional shareholders to communicate and coordinate with each other, and in
2009 it prohibited brokerage firms (which traditionally vote
for incumbent directors) from voting the shares held for their
clients. Another trend that has been especially important in

focusing managerial attention on share price is the use of stock-based compensation. In 1993, Congress amended the tax code to encourage public corporations to tie executive pay to objective "performance" metrics. The percentage of CEO compensation coming from stock option grants then rose from 35 percent in 1994, to over 85 percent by 2001.[85] Finally, whether or not directors and executives of U.S. public companies have an enforceable legal duty to maximize shareholder wealth (Chapter 2 shows they do not), today they are far more likely to *perceive* themselves to have such a duty. In the words of Columbia law professor Jeffrey Gordon, by the 1990s "the maximization of shareholder value as the core test of managerial performance had seeped into managerial culture."[86]

If shareholder value thinking was as good for shareholders as its proponents believe it must be, this collective shift toward more shareholder-oriented governance structures and business practices should have greatly improved average investor returns over the past two decades. Yet we have seen exactly the opposite. Business school dean Roger Martin calculates that between 1933 and 1976 (the year Jensen and Meckling published their article on the principal-agent model), shareholders who invested in the S&P 500 enjoyed real compound average annual returns of 7.5 percent. After 1976, this average dropped to 6.5 percent.[87] The trend is even more apparent if we look at what has happened to public investors since the early 1990s. After an initial run-up in stock prices from 1992 to 1999—fishing with dynamite produces an initial increase in the fish haul, too—shareholder returns have been dismal.

Of course, other factors—financial deregulation, the 2008 credit crisis, and U.S. political dysfunction—may explain shareholders' poor returns in the Age of Shareholder Value. (It is worth noting, however, that shareholder value thinking may have contributed to both financial deregulation and the 2008 crisis, which some attribute to the successful deregulation lobbying efforts of share-price-obsessed firms like Enron and Citibank.)[88] When we look at such a large phenomenon as economic performance, it can be impossible to single out any single cause, or even to identify with certainty a suite of causes. Nevertheless, at a minimum, the stock market's recent performance provides no empirical support for the shareholder primacy thesis.

Shareholder Value Ideology and the Public Company as a Business Form

So let's consider another kind of big-picture evidence on the wisdom of shareholder primacy: corporations' willingness to have public investors at all.

Here too, the evidence suggests that shareholder value thinking may not be working out well for public shareholders. A recent study by consulting firm Grant Thornton concluded that from 1997 to 2009, the number of public companies listed on U.S. stock exchanges has declined by 39 percent in absolute terms, and by a whopping 53 percent when adjusted for GDP growth. Formerly public companies like Toys"R"Us and The Gap are going private, buying back outside investors' shares, and becoming, in effect, closely held companies. Meanwhile private companies, especially start-ups, are reluctant to do initial public offerings (IPOs). According to Grant Thornton, "Small IPOs from all sources—venture capital, private equity and private enterprise—are all nearly extinct and have been for a decade."[89]

Again, there are other explanations one could offer for why the public corporation seems to be increasingly an unattractive form for doing business. Many commentators might lay at least part of the blame on excessive regulation, in particular the much-detested Sarbanes-Oxley requirements imposed by Congress on public firms in the wake of the Enron and Worldcom scandals. Nor, it is important to note, does the slow disappearance of publicly listed companies necessarily herald problems for the U.S. corporate sector in and of itself. After all, private firms are just as capable of producing cars, medicines, and software as public companies are. Indeed, in much of the world (Italy, India, and South America) private companies are more the norm than the exception.

But as we shall see in Part II, there is reason to suspect that the rise of shareholder value plays at least some role in the disappearance of publicly listed companies in which average investors can readily buy shares. This disappearance, in turn, harms those average investors, as they find themselves left with fewer and fewer stocks to choose among in investing and fewer and fewer opportunities to participate in the profits that flow from corporate production.

The Lack of Investor Demand for Shareholder Primacy Rules

As we have already seen, there does not seem to be any particular investor demand for corporate charters that mandate shareholder primacy. But even more compelling, on the rare occasions when companies do go public today, many adopt dual-class equity structures that concentrate voting power and control in insiders' hands. Google, LinkedIn, and Zynga are prominent recent examples. This pattern provides still more evidence against shareholder primacy, because it suggest *public shareholders themselves* do not particularly value shareholder democracy, at least when deciding which firms to buy.

Thanks to the Internet, prospective investors thinking of buying shares in an IPO can easily look to see whether the company's charter strengthens or weakens shareholder rights. They eagerly buy stock in firms like Google that strip them of power. Meanwhile, charter provisions giving shareholders greater leverage over directors—for example by banning poison pill antitakeover defenses—"are so rare as to be almost nonexistent."[90] If public shareholders thought public shareholder oversight and control was essential to good returns, why don't corporations going public try to appeal to investors by offering more shareholder-oriented governance?

Evidence from Abroad

Finally, international comparisons provide a fourth source of evidence to raise doubts about the supposed advantages of shareholder primacy. As we have seen, U.S. law and practice departs substantially from the shareholder primacy ideal. In contrast, the United Kingdom seems a shareholder paradise.[91] Directors in U.K. companies cannot reject hostile takeover bids; they must sit back and let the shareholders decide if the firm will be sold to the highest bidder. Shareholders in U.K. companies have the power to call meetings, and to summarily remove uncooperative directors. They even get to vote to approve dividends. (Not surprisingly, U.K. companies are more generous with dividends than U.S. companies are.)[92]

If the standard model is truly superior, and if corporations run according to the standard model were truly more efficient, the United Kingdom should have the world's best track record in developing successful global public companies. That track record is notably missing. When the average person thinks of great public corporations, the names that come to mind are mostly American, with a few German or Japanese names thrown in: Microsoft, Apple, Walmart, Coca-Cola, Johnson & Johnson, Sony, Toyota, Honda, Canon, Siemens, Bayer, SAP, and Volkswagen.[93] Relatively few U.K. companies have a global profile, and those that do are concentrated in banking (HSBC) and commodities extraction (BP). Moreover, in the wake of the oil spill disaster—which seems to have been due in part to BP's shareholder value obsession—BP's standing in the ranks of global companies has slipped badly.

We Need a New Paradigm

Of course, there are other factors that could explain why the United Kingdom has failed to become a global corporate powerhouse, just as there are other factors one might offer to explain why shareholder returns have declined in recent years, why companies are increasingly reluctant to go or to stay public, and why shareholders eagerly invest in firms that strip away their rights. Because there are so many variables at work when we look at major trends instead of individual companies or nations, statistical regressions of the type so popular among those who do empirical research on corporations may be of little use. Like the drunk who lost his car keys in the dark parking lot but looks for them under the sidewalk lamppost because that's where the light is, researchers who look for the secret of good corporate governance in the economic performance of individual companies are unlikely to meet their objective.

Meanwhile, when we start looking in the dark parking lot, we stumble across some disturbing bits of evidence. The standard model predicts that investors' returns should have improved greatly over the past two decades; that new companies should flock to do business as public corporations; that investors should avoid firms that depart from one-share-one-vote and other shareholder primacy ideals; and that the United States should only now be catching up to the United Kingdom as a leading jurisdiction for global corporations. *None of these predictions has been borne out.* To the contrary, not only does the big picture fail to support shareholder primacy, it suggests, if anything, that shareholder value thinking may be harmful *to shareholders and corporations themselves.*

To use the phrase made famous in Thomas Kuhn's classic book *The Structure of Scientific Revolutions,* by the close of the twentieth century, the shareholder primacy model had become the "dominant paradigm" of corporate purpose. But it fails, rather dramatically, to explain a number of important empirical anomalies. First, U.S. corporate law does not, and never has, required directors of public corporations to maximize shareholder value. Second, closer inspection of the economic structure of public corporations reveals that shareholders are neither owners, nor principals, nor residual claimants. Third, the empirical evidence does not provide clear support for the proposition that shareholder primacy rules produce superior results. Indeed, once we shift our focus from the performance of individual firms to the performance of the corporate sector as a whole, it suggests the opposite.

As Kuhn famously observed, wherever one finds persistent empirical anomalies that are inconsistent with a dominant theory's predictions, sooner or later at least a few free-thinking (or foolhardy) souls will want to understand and explain those anomalies. Eventually these free spirits may develop a new, alternative theory. When they do, the real battle begins. Most of the intellectual leaders who built their careers on the original paradigm can be expected to fight tooth and nail to kill off the newcomer. But if the new theory is sound—if it does a better job of explaining what we observe in the real world than the old theory does—it will win hearts and minds and ultimately prevail. Of course, the process may be slow. It has been said that intellectual progress in science is made one funeral at a time.

New Ideas Emerging

There is reason to hope the pace in corporate theory be more brisk. Even as Hansmann and Kraakman were announcing the triumph of the shareholder wealth maximization paradigm in

2000, pioneering thinkers in law, economics, and business (including Hansmann and Kraakman themselves) were busily at work exploring alternative models of corporate structure and purpose that might better explain corporate reality. Today's literature includes several compelling lines of thought that challenge traditional shareholder primacy.

The next part (Part II) explores some of these emerging theories and shows how they uncover and illuminate the pitfalls of shareholder primacy thinking. In particular, Part II focuses on intellectual challenges to traditional shareholder primacy thinking that have three important characteristics in common.

First, the new theories differ from the traditional stakeholder and corporate social responsibility arguments against maximizing shareholder value, because they focus not on how shareholder primacy hurts stakeholders or society *per se*, but on how shareholder primacy can hurt *shareholders*, both individually and immediately, and collectively and over time. This focus on shareholder welfare may not fully satisfy those who believe that directors and executives of public corporations should use their control over corporate resources to promote social justice, employee well-being, or environmental health as goods in and of themselves. But they do suggest, strongly, that the supposed divides between the interests of shareholders and the interests of stakeholders, society, and the environment maybe much narrower than conventional shareholder value thinking admits. Public corporations are more likely to do well for their investors when they do good.

Second, the theories examined in Part II have in common that they pay much more careful attention to the idea of "the shareholder." Many people think of corporations as fictions and shareholders as real. This perception explains much of the appeal of the principal-agent model, which appears to clear away the fog of corporate identity by focusing on the apparent reality of human agents. Yet corporations *are* real, at least in legal sense. *It is shareholders that are fictional.* The standard shareholder-oriented model assumes a hypothetical, homogeneous, abstract shareholder who does not and cannot exist. In his place stand real human beings who happen to own shares of stock. These real human beings have different investing time frames; different liquidity demands; different interests in other assets (including their own human capital); and different attitudes toward whether they should live their lives without regard for others or behave "prosocially." Recognizing these differences reveals that the idea of a single objectively measurable "shareholder value" is not only quixotic, but intellectually incoherent.

Third and perhaps most important, by recognizing the differences between and among shareholders' interests, the new models *explain empirical anomalies the standard model cannot.* The new models are better inductively, meaning they do a better job of predicting the empirical data we observe. They are also better deductively, meaning they explain how and why such "anomalies" persist. In a Kuhnian sense, they are better paradigms for understanding public corporations.

This means that, by demanding that corporations maximize shareholder value, we may indeed be fishing with dynamite. It is not only logically possible, but predictable, that a single-minded focus on maximizing "shareholder wealth" can end up harming shareholders—and stakeholders, corporations, society, and the environment as well.

PART II

What Do Shareholders Really Value?

CHAPTER 5

Short-Term Speculators versus Long-Term Investors

Of all the possible problems posed when corporations adopt "maximize shareholder value" as their goal, one in particular has captured the attention of the business community almost from the beginning of the standard model's ascendance. This is the fear that companies whose directors focus on stock price will run firms in ways that raise that price in the short term, but harm firms' long-term prospects. For example, a company might seek to raise accounting profits by eliminating research and development expenses, or cutting back on customer relations and support in ways that eventually erode consumer trust and brand loyalty. The result is a kind of corporate myopia that reduces long-term returns from stock ownership.

Beyond the Efficient Market Hypothesis

Until 1987, many finance economists argued that the myopia argument made no sense, because it was impossible for managers to adopt strategies that harmed the firm's future without producing an immediate decline in share price. This argument was based on widespread embrace of a theory called the "efficient markets hypothesis."[94] Although the literature on the efficient markets hypothesis is both enormous and technical enough to induce narcolepsy, the basic idea can be summarized as follows: stock markets are "fundamental value efficient" when the market price of a company's stock incorporates all information relevant to its value, producing a share price that reflects the best possible rational estimate of the stock's likely future risks and returns. In a fundamental value efficient market, there is no need for an investor to stay up late at night trying to figure out what her shares are really worth. She can sleep soundly knowing the market has done her valuation homework for her. Nor is there any fear that today's stock price might not reflect the firm's long-run value. Long run and short run merge, because there is only one accurate way to measure a stock's future risks and returns: by its current market price. Corporate myopia cannot be a problem, because the stock market punishes shortsightedness.

Even during the 1970s and early 1980s, the heyday of efficient market theory, many CEOs, directors, and professional investors had their doubts about whether stock prices really captured fundamental value. Even finance theorists understood there were some limits to market efficiency. For example, absent rampant insider trading, private information that is available only to corporate insiders (say, news that a promising new drug for male pattern baldness has just been discovered to cause impotence) might not be fully reflected in stock price until the bad news is made public.

But collective confidence in the accuracy of stock market prices was shattered on October 19, 1987. On that day, the Dow Jones industrial average inexplicably lost 23 percent of its value in a single trading session. (The value appeared again, equally mysteriously, a few months later.) The tech stock bubble of the late 1990s further undermined trust in market prices, as did companies like Enron and Global Crossing, whose stock price soared beyond any sane estimate of value before crashing spectacularly.

It is nearly impossible today to find a finance economist under the age of fifty who would claim stock market prices *always* capture true value. Indeed, many respected theorists now occupy themselves exploring alternatives to efficient market theory that can explain how markets go wrong. These alternatives include "heterogeneous expectations" models that incorporate the possibility of investor disagreement; new work on the "limits of arbitrage" that explains how some information gets incorporated into prices only slowly and incompletely; and the burgeoning field of "behavioral finance," which examines how human emotions and irrationalities can distort prices and drive trading.[95]

If the idea that stock prices always reflect true value is not entirely dead, it is at least seriously wounded. (Economist John Quiggen calls it a "zombie" idea, neither living nor quite dead.)[96] But substantial support remains for the claim that—barring unusual circumstances and occasional fits of collective investor irrationality—over the long run, stock prices tend to be reasonably related to actual values. In the words of famed finance professor Fischer Black, many experts might argue that the market is efficient in the sense that "price is within a factor of [two] of value, i.e., the price is more than half of value and less than twice value."[97]

For many shareholder primacy enthusiasts, this is good enough. They argue that shareholders still benefit when managers look to share price as their guiding star, because even if the market temporarily misvalues companies, mistakes correct themselves over time. Thus shareholders themselves have reason to try to prevent managerial myopia: they understand that pressuring managers to raise share price through strategies that harm the company's future will likely end up hurting the value of their own shares.

This view ignores an inconvenient reality. Long-term shareholders fear corporate myopia. *Short-term shareholders embrace it—and many powerful shareholders today are short-term shareholders.*

The Role of Short-Term Investors in Today's Stock Market

To understand just how hyperactive today's stock markets have become, consider that in 1960, annual share turnover for firms listed on the New York Stock Exchange (NYSE) was only 12 percent, implying an average holding period of about eight years. By 1987, this figure had risen to 73 percent.[98] By 2010, the average annual turnover for equities listed on U.S. exchanges reached an astonishing 300 percent annually, implying an average holding period of only four months.[99]

This is a very odd phenomenon. At the end of the day, most stocks are held either by individuals with long-term investing goals (like saving for retirement or for a child's college tuition), or by institutions like pension funds and mutual funds that run portfolios on behalf of these individuals.[100] Even hedge fund clients are typically pension funds, universities, and foundations looking for steady, long-run returns on their endowments.

If most investors want long-term results for themselves or for their clients, why is there so much more short-term trading? Part of the answer lies in the fact that deregulation and advances in information technology have made stock trading much cheaper than it used to be. Once upon a time, someone who thought a particular stock was under- or overpriced had to call a broker, pay a fixed commission, and possibly pay a transfer tax as well to trade. High transactions costs discouraged hyperactive trading. Now trading has become so inexpensive that some funds specialize in computerized "flash trading" strategies in which shares are bought and held for mere seconds before being sold again.

But another very important part of the short-term equation, emphasized in a recent report from the Aspen Institute, is the growing role that institutional investors like mutual funds, pension funds, and hedge funds play in the market.[101] As already noted, such funds mostly invest on behalf of individuals with long-term goals. Unfortunately, these individual clients tend to judge the fund managers to whom they have outsourced their investing decisions based on their most recent investing records. This explains why many actively-managed mutual funds turn over 100 percent or more of their equity portfolios annually and why "activist" hedge funds that purport to make long-term investments in improving corporate performance typically hold shares for less than two years. The mutual fund manager whose continued employment depends on her relative performance for the next four quarters finds it hard to resist the temptation to support management strategies that will raise share price just long enough that she can sell and move on to the next stock that might see a short-term bump in its stock. As mutual fund guru and Vanguard Funds founder Jack Bogle puts it, the mutual fund industry has become a "rent-a-stock" industry.[102]

Short-Term Shareholders Push for Short-Term Results

The result is that mutual funds and hedge funds pressure directors and executives to pursue myopic business strategies that don't add lasting value. For example, the information arbitrage literature suggests that when information is public but not widely available, or is technical and difficult to understand, it filters into market prices relatively slowly.[103] Thus cutting expenses by firing employees or reducing customer support may produce a short-term bump in stock price because the market understands immediately that corporate expenses have been reduced but is slow to see the negative long-term impact of employee disaffection or weakening brand loyalty. One recent survey of 400 corporate finance officers found that a full 80 percent reported they would cut expenses like marketing or product development to make their quarterly earnings targets, even if they knew the likely result was to hurt long-term corporate performance.[104]

An even better way to raise share price without improving real performance is old-fashioned accounting fraud. The market eventually figured out that Enron and Worldcom were cooking their books. But for several years, institutional investors profited as Enron and Worldcom executives "unlocked" enough shareholder value to make those who sold some or all of their shares before the frauds were discovered quite rich. For example, suppose a mutual fund invested $100,000 in Enron stock in 1993, when it was trading at just over $10 per share. Then suppose, realistically, the fund sold some of its Enron holdings each year as Enron's price skyrocketed upward, in order to maintain fund diversification. By 2000, when Enron was trading over $90 per share, the fund might have earned a profit many times larger than its initial $100,000 investment—even if it still owned $100,000 in Enron stock when the company cratered in 2001. Financial fraud is not bad for all investors, only for those unlucky investors who buy and hold most of their shares until after the fraud is discovered.

"Heterogeneous expectations" asset-pricing models (which differ from conventional financial-pricing models by assuming, realistically, that people disagree about the future) also suggest a number of "financial engineering" tricks that short-term investors can push corporate managers to adopt to raise share price without improving long-term performance. For example, practical and legal limits on short selling ensure that the shares of any particular company are typically held, and market price set by, investors who are relatively optimistic about that company's future. By making a large share repurchase on the open market, the company can shrink its pool of shareholders until price is set only by the *wildly* optimistic. For similar reasons, a sale of the entire company—which typically requires a buyer to purchase shares not only from the relative realists in the shareholder pool but from the more-optimistic as well—usually demands that the bidder pay a substantial premium over market price.[105] As yet another example, splitting up companies by selling off assets or divisions can create "shareholder value" by allowing different investors to invest only in the particular line of business they favor most. It's much easier to be wildly optimistic about the future of a single product or division than the fate of a conglomerate that sells everything from pet food to airplane engines to financial services.

Different Time Frames, Clashing Interests

Once we recognize that stock markets are not perfectly fundamental value efficient and that managers can raise share price without improving real economic performance, we also have to recognize that shareholders with different investing time horizons have conflicting interests. The shareholder who plans to hold her stock for many years wants the company to invest in its employees' skills, develop new products, build good working relationships with suppliers, and take care of customers to build consumer trust and brand loyalty—even if the value of these investments in the future is not immediately reflected in share price. The short-term investor who expects to hold for only a few months or days wants to raise share today, and favors strategies like cutting expenses, using cash reserves to repurchase shares, and selling assets or even the entire company. An important empirical study of activist hedge funds by Bill Bratton at the University of Pennsylvania confirms these are exactly the strategies activist funds demand. In Bratton's words, "Activist hedge funds look for four things in their targets—potential sale of the whole, potential sale of a part, free cash, and cuttable costs."[106]

This poses a dilemma for the standard shareholder-oriented model. *Toward which shareholders is it oriented?* If stock prices do not always capture fundamental value, a conflict of interest exists between long-term investors who want directors to invest in the company's future, and short-term investors, especially activist hedge funds, who simply want to raise share price today. In the words of corporate lawyer Martin Lipton, directors must decide "whether the long-term interests of the nation's corporate system and economy should be jeopardized in order to benefit speculators interested not in the vitality and continued existence of the business enterprises in which they have bought shares, but only in a quick profit on the sale of those shares?"[107]

Lipton's language makes clear he's on the side of the long-term investors, not the short-term speculators. I share his view, but I do not attempt in this book to provide a definitive answer to the difficult question of when and how directors should favor the interests of one kind of shareholder over those of another. The most important thing is to recognize that *long-term investors and short-term activist hedge funds do not compete on a level playing field.* Activist hedge funds have the clear advantage, because they concentrate their investment portfolios into just a few securities. This means it is worth their while to spend the time and effort necessary to become involved in a particular firm's affairs. Diversified retail investors, by contrast, rarely have a big enough stake in any single company to make it sensible to closely monitor what's going on; they suffer from their own rational apathy. Mutual funds are not much better. Most fund managers rationally conclude it is not in their clients' interests for them to exercise an active governance role in the dozens or even hundreds of firms whose stocks the fund manager keeps in his portfolio. If there's a problem, the fund manager will do the "Wall Street Walk" and sell the shares quickly and quietly, before anyone else catches on. As a result, mutual fund managers mostly vote the shares they hold as directed by RiskMetrics' Institutional Shareholder Services (ISS), a "proxy advisory service" whose ideas about good corporate governance can be criticized for focusing on short-term stock price performance.[108] The end result is that the only shareholders that are likely to engage in any serious way with incumbent management are hedge funds and ISS-shepherded mutual funds, both of which are biased toward the short term.

Managing Shareholder Value Means Managing Expectations

Finally, in his 2011 book *Fixing the Game*, business school dean Roger Martin has pointed out yet another reason why measuring corporate success by stock price ends up harming long-term shareholders: because it drives directors and executives to focus not on real corporate performance (sales, revenues, growth, new products) but on what Martin dubs "the expectations market":

> The expectations market is the world in which shares in companies are traded between investors—in other words, the stock market. In this market, investors assess the real market activities of a company today and, on the basis of that assessment, form expectations as to how the company is likely to perform in the future. The consensus view of all investors and potential investors as to the expectations of future performance shapes the stock price of the company.[109]

According to Martin, using the expectations market to gauge performance—especially when this is done by compensating CEOs and other executives primarily with options, stock grants, or bonuses tied to share price—puts executives in a terrible bind. Suppose a company is doing well; the firm is operating at peak performance and looks as if it can hum along at peak performance indefinitely. The stock market will incorporate this expectation of optimal future performance into today's stock price. How then can a CEO raise stock prices any further?

In Martin's words, "Modern capitalism dictates that the job of executive leadership is to maximize shareholder value, as measured by the market value of the company's stock. To that end, the CEO should always be working to increase the stock price, to raise expectations about the company's stock price ad infinitum . . . the lesson is that no matter how good you are, you cannot beat expectations forever."[110] Focusing on shareholder value gives managers "a task that is ultimately unachievable, in that it requires that they raise other people's expectations continuously and forever."[111]

What's a CEO to do? If she is a mere mortal, she may decide not to attempt the unachievable but instead to do the achievable: manage expectations, for example by using accounting manipulations ("earnings management") to produce one disastrous quarter that dramatically lowers and resets the market's expectations, so she can raise expectations again thereafter. Alternatively, she may elect to avoid the slow, hard, thankless task of developing new products, hiring new employees, and increasing sales and profits, and focus instead on cost-cutting (firing employees, reducing R&D) or financial engineering (selling off assets, making massive share repurchases) that temporarily raises stock prices without adding real long-term value.

Stock-based compensation schemes thus create an unhealthy alliance between short-term institutional investors like activist hedge funds and ISS-advised mutual funds who move in and out of stocks, and executives whose compensation plans drive them to focus obsessively on stock market expectations. Consider the case of Kraft Foods. In 2010, Kraft completed a controversial takeover of iconic British candy manufacturer Cadbury, causing the disappearance of one of the United Kingdom's few internationally recognized non-financial companies. Only 18 months later, under pressure from hedge fund shareholders, Kraft is now planning to split itself into two companies again. One will sell snack foods like Oreos cookies and Cadbury chocolate, and the other will sell grocery staples like Oscar Meyer cold cuts and Kraft macaroni and cheese. The split seems unlikely to result in any dramatic changes in the way the company manufactures or markets chocolates and cold cuts, although it might produce some duplication of expenses. Nevertheless, Kraft's hedge-fund shareholders and stock-compensated executives can reasonably hope that splitting the company in two will "unlock shareholder value" by allowing the price for a one business to be set only by investors who are optimistic about the future of sugar-laden snack foods, while the other is set by investors bullish on basic groceries.[112]

Such games of corporate musical chairs would not be a problem if they allowed executives and short-term speculators to profit without harming anyone else. Unfortunately, long-term investors have to eat the short-termers' cooking. There are signs the meal is not sitting well. The SEC does not require unregulated hedge funds to publicly disclose their results, so it can be hard to find solid data on hedge fund performance, but there is some evidence activist hedge funds in particular outperform the market.[113] And there is little doubt that stock-based compensation schemes have made executives much wealthier over the past two decades. Meanwhile, average investors' returns have languished. Even as a laser-like focus on "unlocking shareholder value" has enriched executives and some hedge fund managers, it has done little or nothing to help shareholders as a class.

When long-term and short-term investors' interests diverge, shareholder value thinking poses the same risks as fishing with dynamite. Some individuals may reap immediate and dramatic returns. But over time and as a whole, investors and the economy lose.

CHAPTER 6

Keeping Promises to Build Successful Companies

We have just seen how, when stock market prices don't capture fundamental value perfectly, the interests of short-term speculators conflict with those of longer-term investors. This chapter examines an even odder chronological tension: the conflict between shareholders' initial interest in making commitments to stakeholders and to each other, and their subsequent interest in breaking those commitments later.

To understand the nature of the problem, consider Ulysses's dilemma when he sailed the *Odyssey* past the island of the Sirens. The Sirens were beautiful women with compelling voices, but like many beautiful women they followed a strict diet: they used their singing to lure sailors to the island, where the Sirens would promptly kill and eat them. To protect his men from the Sirens' songs, Ulysses ordered them to stuff their ears with wax as the *Odyssey* sailed by the island, so they could not hear. But Ulysses himself wanted to experience the Sirens' music. He left his ears unplugged and ordered his sailors to bind him tightly to the *Odyssey's* mast. He also told his sailors not to release him, no matter how he begged and pleaded, until after the Sirens were safely out of sight and sound.

Before approaching the Sirens' island—"ex ante," as academics put it—Ulysses wanted above all to make sure that he escaped the Siren's clutches. "Ex post," while actually listening to the Sirens' music, Ulysses wanted nothing more than to jump overboard, swim to the island, and present himself as that day's entrée. Luckily, ex ante Ulysses figured out a way to make sure ex post Ulysses did not succumb to the Sirens' charms. He had himself "bound to the mast" (as we say today, "tied his own hands") to protect himself from his own future behavior.

The Shareholder as Ulysses

Shareholders do much the same when they buy stock in public corporations. When equity investors buy stock in the "primary market" where companies raise capital by selling shares, the investors' money instantly becomes the *corporation's* money. All the equity investor owns now is a contract with the corporate entity, called "a share of stock." This contract does not entitle the stockholder to get her money back. She may or may not get dividends, depending on what the directors decide; she may or may not find another investor willing to purchase her contract in the "secondary market" where investors buy from and sell stock to each other. But her initial capital contribution is, to use the words of influential corporate scholar Margaret Blair at Vanderbilt, "locked in" to the corporate entity. Shareholders have no legal right to demand their money back, in whole or in part. Corporations aren't like partnerships, where a partner at any time can leave the partnership and get back her proportionate share of the partnership's assets.

For most of the twentieth century, the phenomenon of capital lock-in received little scholarly attention. Business and law school professors routinely taught their students that corporations were attractive ways to do business primarily because they offered shareholders four characteristics: (1) limited personal liability, (2) centralized management, (3) indefinite legal life, and (in the case of public corporations) (4) liquid stock markets where investors could sell their shares.

This fourth characteristic, in particular, obscured the reality of capital lock-in by creating an illusion that equity investments in public corporations were liquid and could be easily withdrawn. But stocks are only liquid *on the margin.* Should all a firm's shareholders decide to sell at once—say, because the CEO is indicted, or the company is struggling—the liquidity illusion quickly disappears. Shareholders discover to their horror a fifth characteristic of corporations: their money is locked in and inaccessible.

So why would any sane investor buy stock in a public corporation? Why not stick to partnerships and other business forms that allow you to get your cash back whenever you demand it?

Some Advantages of Tying Your Hands

This question was perhaps first raised in print by UCLA economist Harold Demsetz, who noted in 1995 that a "largely unrecognized" condition of share ownership in public companies was "the inability of investors to force the firm to disgorge assets purchased with funds secured for the initial sale of stock."[114] Demsetz then observed:

> It is impractical from the perspective of being able to make business commitments to allow shareholders to reclaim their share of the firm's assets in the typical case. The corporation makes commitments to purchase materials and plant, as well as to provide goods and services. If these commitments are to be treated as reliable, the firm must have control of the asset it has secured through the sale of stock or bonds. It cannot be in continual jeopardy of losing assets to its disappointed shareholders. The typical corporation must be organized in a way that bars investors from reclaiming their fraction of the firm's assets in other than exceptional circumstances. The firm is, therefore, granted a life that is in important ways distinct from the lives and desires of those who supply it with capital and other inputs.[115]

Other scholars have expanded on Demsetz's insight in ways that cut directly against shareholder value thinking. They have shown how shareholder-oriented governance rules that allow shareholders to withdraw their funds—including rules that make it easier for shareholders to pressure boards to pay dividends or implement share repurchase programs— can actually reduce shareholder wealth by discouraging *other* financial and nonfinancial investors from making important "firm-specific" contributions to corporate production.

For example, in her 2003 historical analysis of the rise of the corporate form, Margaret Blair described how capital lock-in protects shareholders from the impecuniousness and opportunism of their fellow shareholders.[116] Suppose you want to build a canal or a factory. The project requires more funds than any single investor could, or would want, to put up, so several investors agree to contribute together. If they organize as a partnership, they face a serious problem. What if one of the investors wants his money back, perhaps because he has fallen on hard times? What if a partner dies and her heirs don't want to take her place in the business, but instead cash in their inheritance? You can't sell off pieces of a canal or factory without destroying much of its value. Factories and canals are "firm-specific" investments, resources that can't be easily withdrawn from the firm without destroying at least part of their value.

A partnership is no way to build a canal or factory. But if our four investors incorporate, the firm-specific canal or factory will now belong to the corporate entity itself. No single shareholder can demand back her share of the company's assets. This protects the four investors from each other's possible future poverty. It also protects the four investors from the siren song of opportunism.

More Advantages: Discouraging Opportunism

To see how lock-in protects against opportunism, suppose the four investors agreed to form a partnership to build the canal or factory, and also agreed each partner would receive 25 percent of any future profits. After the canal or factory is built, one of the four might demand that, unless the partnership agreement was amended to give her 50 percent of profits, she would withdraw from the partnership and take her one-fourth of the canal or factory with her. The threat is self-destructive but effective, like a bank robber's threat to blow up himself and the bank unless the teller follows his instructions.

The incentive to attempt such holdups is greatly reduced if the four investors incorporate their business. Now, the canal or factory is owned by, and locked into, the corporate entity. No single shareholder can threaten to withdraw her capital and unilaterally blow up the business. The corporation's board of directors decides when and if shareholders will receive any dividends, and it would take three of the four shareholders to replace the board.

The need to discourage investor opportunism becomes even more obvious when we look at the role of bondholders and other creditors. If bondholders could demand their money back from the corporation at any time, no firm could safely use borrowed money to make long-term investments. Conversely, if shareholders were free to withdraw capital from the corporation at any time, no sensible creditor would ever lend to a corporation, for fear the shareholders would simply use the borrowed money to pay themselves a massive dividend, leaving the firm insolvent and the creditor holding the bag. Moreover, even if the shareholders are by law or contract constrained in paying themselves dividends (as they generally are), without capital lock-in, the corporation's creditors still have to worry about *shareholders'* creditors, and the possibility that a bankrupt shareholder's creditors might try to recover from the corporation itself the value of the shareholder's interest in the firm.

This last point was explored in some detail by Hansmann and Kraakman in an article they published in 2000, just before their influential "End of History" essay proclaimed the triumph of shareholder primacy ideology. Hansmann and Kraakman examined what they call corporate asset shielding, the corporation's ability to protect its assets from the claims of shareholders and shareholders' creditors. They argued that asset shielding is essential in business projects where "partial or complete liquidation of the firm's assets could destroy some or all of the firm's going concern value," because "a [shareholder's] personal creditor with the right to foreclose on firm assets might well threaten to exercise that right and destroy substantial going concern value—even if he could realize little or nothing thereby because the firm lacks sufficient net worth—simply to hold up the firm (or its owners or creditors) for a sum larger than his claim on the firm would receive if he actually foreclosed."[117]

Blair's discussion of capital lock-in, and Hansmann's and Kraakman's work on asset shielding, both illustrate how conventional shareholder primacy rules that may seem to benefit shareholders ex post by allowing them to "unlock" their financial capital from the corporation, can actually harm them ex ante by making it harder for business enterprises to get started in the first place. Only when financial capital can be made secure from the demands of shareholders and creditors alike, can it be safely used to make firm-specific investments in complex, uncertain, long-range projects—constructing railroads, canals, and factories, developing new drugs, software and technologies, building trusted brand names.

Still More Advantages: Encouraging Stakeholder Investment

But a corporation's need for firm-specific investment is not limited to financial capital. In a 1999 article, Margaret Blair and I developed a more general theory of the role of firm-specific investments in corporate governance that we call the team production theory.[118] Economists say a project requires "team production" whenever two or more actors must make specific contributions that are essential to the project's success, and that can't be withdrawn from the project without losing much of their value. Moving a large sofa is a classic example of team production. Two or more people are needed, and if one quits in the middle, the "sofa-moving specific" efforts of all are wasted.

Many successful corporate projects require team production with stakeholders, meaning they demand not only locked-in capital from financial investors (whose money becomes firm-specific after being spent on salaries, specialized equipment, and other nonrecoverable expenses) but also specific investment from employees, customers, and even the community. For example, a railroad needs more than a set of tracks and some empty railroad cars. It also needs employees with specialized skills (engineering, conducting) who live in the area; commuting customers who have decided to live and work along the railroad line; and local communities to build and maintain roads, parking lots, schools, power grids, and other vital infrastructure along the line. None of these essential stakeholders would make such firm-specific investments if they thought the railroad might disappear tomorrow—as it might, if creditors or shareholders could easily and unilaterally withdraw their financial contributions.

As Blair and I discuss at length in our 1999 article, this insight explains a host of otherwise-puzzling anomalies in American corporate law that can't be explained by the standard shareholder-oriented model, including the rules of derivative suit procedure, the nature of fiduciary duties, and shareholders' extremely limited voting rights. Most important, it explains the peculiar institution of the board of directors. Economists since Adam Smith have wondered why sane investors would cede control over their hard-earned cash to strangers. (This is exactly what happens when you buy stock in a public corporation.) The answer, Blair and I suggest, is not that investors expect boards to run corporations perfectly, or even particularly well. But they do expect directors to run the public company well enough to keep the firm on its feet, else they would lose their own board positions. They also expect directors not to steal corporate assets: corporate law's duty of loyalty has real teeth, and severely limits directors' discretion to use their corporate powers to enrich themselves. Meanwhile, by relinquishing control of corporate assets to boards, financial investors get a valuable consolation prize. Board control allows directors to act as "mediating hierarchs" who can balance the ex post demands of shareholders against the interests of other stakeholders—customers, suppliers, employees, the community—that make essential contributions to firms. This reassures stakeholders and makes it safer for them to make their own firm-specific investments, which in turn allows the firm to pursue profitable projects it otherwise could not.

Some Evidence of Investor Hands-Tying

The corporation's need to encourage firm-specific investments from employees and other stakeholders explains an interesting empirical puzzle that is impossible to reconcile with conventional shareholder primacy. This puzzle is the contrast between investors' apparent willingness to buy stock in firms with governance rules that reduce shareholder power, while complaining about similar rules at other firms in which they own shares. Why would the same mutual fund manager buy shares in a company with a staggered board, while dutifully voting with ISS to try to de-stagger the boards of other companies in the manager's portfolio? [119] Why not just avoid buying stock in companies that limit shareholder power in the first place?

Ulysses's tale suggests an answer. When corporations pursue complex, long-term projects with uncertain results —building brand names, inventing new technologies, developing new drugs or software—they often depend critically on their employees' creativity, dedication, and passion. Unfortunately, it's hard to draft employment contracts that guarantee creativity, dedication, and passion. Instead, corporations can encourage employee firm-specific investment by trying to reassure employees their investments will be respected and protected. Placing control of the project and its profits in the hands of a board that cannot personally profit from withdrawing financial capital or opportunistically threatening stakeholders (as shareholders can) helps provide that reassurance. Staggered board provisions and dual-class equity schemes that make it harder for an opportunistic shareholder to oust the board provide additional protection. Thus, governance provisions like staggered boards or dual classes of shares make some kinds of corporate projects more likely to succeed, in turn making corporations with those governance structures more attractive investments.

Of course, when listening to the Sirens, Ulysses wanted his hands unbound. Similarly, once a corporation's stakeholders have made essential firm-specific investments in the company's success, its shareholders might want to exploit that stakeholder trust and vulnerability. For example, a firm might try to raise profits by threatening to outsource manufacturing to China or India unless its employees accept lower wages and the local community provides larger tax breaks.

In contrast, the duty of loyalty prevents directors from reaping personal profits by exploiting stakeholders. With no reason to try to exploit stakeholders, the board may resist shareholder demands to behave opportunistically. But what if the shareholders can easily remove the board, perhaps by selling en masse to a takeover bidder who would become a majority shareholder who did not suffer from collective action problems? Now, shareholders are in a much better position to demand the board try to profit from exploiting employees' specific investments. (Economists Andrei Shleifer and Lawrence Summers estimated that after Carl Icahn acquired TWA in a takeover that earned TWA shareholders a premium of about $300 to $400 million, TWA's unionized employees lost about $800 million in future wages.)[120] This explains why the development of an active hostile takeover market in the 1980s was accompanied by labor force reductions (which hurt employees) and increased leverage (which harmed creditors).

Another tragedy of the investing commons results. Stakeholders eventually cotton on to what shareholders are doing, and become reluctant to make firm-specific contributions to public corporations subject to shareholder primacy pressures. Instead, they prefer making firm-specific investments in private corporations with controlling shareholders who have shown personal trustworthiness (there is evidence that corporations with more entrenched boards take better care of their employees and are more socially responsible), or not at all.[121]

Shareholder Value Thinking Discourages Team Production

Shareholder value thinking thus changes potential stakeholders' perceptions of public corporations in ways that make it harder to pursue projects that require team production. There is some evidence this is occurring. Surveys report that as U.S. firms have embraced the ideology of shareholder primacy, employee loyalty has declined.[122] Similarly, as noted in the Introduction, the number of U.S. public corporations has dropped dramatically as public firms "go private," and many new companies opt not to go public at all.

Further support for this thesis can be found in the empirical observation, mentioned in Chapter 5, that the United Kingdom's relatively few global corporations are concentrated in finance and commodities extraction, especially minerals, oil, and gas production.[123] This pattern may be driven by the United Kingdom's relatively shareholder-friendly laws (for example, shareholders vote on dividends and can more easily remove directors). These laws make it more difficult for U.K. corporations to lock in shareholder capital. For example, under pressure from the American government in the wake of the *Deepwater Horizon* oil spill, BP announced it would suspend paying its regular dividends. This sparked a firestorm of protests from British pensioners who relied on BP dividends for retirement income. BP agreed to quickly resume paying dividends after announcing plans to sell off approximately $30 billion in assets, including many BP oil fields.

BP's reluctance to suspend dividends for more than a short period of time, and its willingness to sell off assets rather than disappoint its shareholders, illustrates how greater shareholder primacy means less ability to lock in corporate capital in a fashion that protects stakeholders. This likely explains why U.K. public companies concentrate in finance and commodities extraction. Neither industry demands much firm-specific investment. Productive mines and oil fields are not firm-specific because, as BP's asset sales show, they can be sold off fairly easily for full value. Finance requires money and people, but money is not firm-specific: a dollar is worth the same to HSBC and Barclays. Nor do finance employees invest much in firm-specific human capital. Goldman Sachs investment bankers and Morgan Stanley traders can easily take their skills and their client relationships to other banks, and often do, and at least in the United States, any attempt to stop them would run afoul of the U.S. Constitution's Thirteenth Amendment.

Shareholder value thinking, which is even more prevalent in the United Kingdom than in the United States, may have prevented the U.K. business sector from developing much beyond finance and commodities extraction. One can argue that because the United Kingdom is a relatively small economy, it can afford to keep most of its economic eggs in the finance and commodities extraction baskets. (Some pensioners in the United Kingdom might beg to differ: before the spill, BP dividends accounted for nearly 15 percent of all dividends paid by U.K. firms).[124] But such extreme specialization is not a viable strategy for a nation as large as the United States, nor for the global economy as a whole. Someone, somewhere, needs to build cars, ships and airplanes; research new drugs and medical devices; develop new software and information technologies; and create trusted brand names to sell televisions, computers, and breakfast cereals.

Team production theory teaches that such businesses cannot thrive if they are run according to shareholder primacy ideology. There is an inevitable conflict between shareholders' ex ante interest in "tying their own hands" to encourage their own and other stakeholders' firm-specific contributions, and their ex post interest in opportunistically trying to unbind themselves to unlock capital and exploit others' specific contributions. This conflict—a conflict between shareholders' ex ante selves and their ex post selves, if you will—puts public corporations governed by the rules of shareholder primacy at a disadvantage when it comes to projects that require firm-specific investments. Rejecting shareholder value thinking, and instead inviting boards to consider the needs of employees, customers, and communities, allows boards to usefully mediate not only between the interests of shareholders and stakeholders, but between the interests of ex ante and ex post shareholders as well.

CHAPTER 7

Hedge Funds versus Universal Investors

To most people, corporations are abstractions. As one old English case famously put it, corporations have "no soul to damn and no body to kick." By contrast, shareholders seem concrete. When we imagine shareholders, we picture parents saving for a child's college tuition; retirees waiting for dividend checks; or, sometimes, a wealthy hedge fund baron driving his Ferrari up a long driveway between manicured lawns to the door of his Connecticut mansion.

Corporations Are Real, Shareholders Are Fictions

This view gets it backwards. Corporations may be invisible, but they are quite real. Corporations own real property, enter real contracts, and pay real damages for committing real torts. They can live indefinitely, control more resources than many national governments, and thrive, weed-like, in the harshest locations and climates. By contrast, "the shareholder" is fictional. Shareholders seem more real than corporations because when we think of shareholders, we are not actually thinking of shareholders at all. We are thinking of human beings: fragile biological organisms who may happen to own, among their many different assets, shares of stock.

The standard shareholder primacy model judges corporate performance from the perspective of something that does not exist: an entity whose only goal is to maximize the market price of the shares of a single company. In reality, even institutional investors like pension funds and mutual funds practice diversification. Their portfolios include shares in other companies, corporate bonds, preferred stock, real estate, and other types of investments as well. Moreover, these institutions themselves exist to serve the interests of their human beneficiaries, who often have their own investments in homes, real estate, and bank deposits. Indeed, for many beneficiaries their biggest investment is in their own human capital: their health, education, and earnings from employment. And humans, whether they hold stocks directly or through mutual and pension funds, are not just investors. They are also consumers who buy products, citizens who pay taxes, and organisms that breathe air and drink water.

External Costs Are a Problem for Universal Owners

This basic insight underlies an important intellectual challenge to shareholder value thinking: the idea of the "universal owner" or "universal investor." Shareholder value thinking looks at the world from the perspective of a Platonic investor whose only asset is equity shares in one firm (say, BP) and whose only purpose and desire in life is to raise today's price for BP shares by any means possible. But this Platonic shareholder does not exist. Real human beings own BP's shares, either directly or indirectly through pension and mutual funds, and real human beings care about much more than just whether BP stock rises. They also want to protect the value of their other investments, keep their jobs, lower their tax bills, and preserve their health. They are to, a greater or lesser extent, "universal owners" with stakes in the economy, the community, and the planet.

Consider someone who owns not only BP stock, but also holds BP bonds; owns shares in other oil companies; owns a beach home on the Florida Panhandle; has a job in the Gulf tourism industry; and values his own human capital, includ-ing his good physical health and social connections in a thriv-ing coastal community. By skimping on safety corners, BP may have given this investor several years of above-average share performance. But by causing an enormous oil spill in the Gulf, BP's risk-taking imposed much greater "external costs" on the investor's other interests. As a result of the *Deepwater Horizon* disaster, the U.S. government imposed a moratorium on exploratory drilling in the Gulf that idled not only BP's op-erations but those of other oil companies as well. The spill hurt the value of BP bonds, which were downgraded in the disaster's wake. The value of beachfront property in the Gulf declined, and its tourism and fishing industries suffered. The Gulf ecosystem was harmed, and its ability to provide healthy seafood and safe recreation degraded.

BP provides only one example of how companies can "cre-ate" shareholder value through strategies that impose larger external costs on universal investors. There are many others. For example, a software company like Microsoft or Oracle might increase profits by buying out or destroying its rivals, thus gaining monopoly power that allows it to raise the price of its products. Unfortunately, if its shareholders are also software consumers, those monopoly profits come from the shareholders' pockets. A Verizon or Hewlett-Packard might raise its share price by cutting employee wages or health benefits, or simply cutting employees, but when American companies embrace this approach en masse, American inves-tors who are also employees suffer. GE may lobby for legal loopholes to avoid paying corporate taxes, but when corpora-tions pay no taxes, humans must either pay more taxes, or go without government services.

Finally, it is well understood that the shareholders of a target company in a takeover or merger typically see their wealth increase when they receive a premium over the origi-nal market price for their shares. But numerous studies have also shown that, even as the shareholders of a target company receive a premium, the shares of the bidding company, which is typically much larger, often lose value.[125] As a result, the gains to the shareholders of acquired firms in mergers and takeovers can be outweighed by larger losses to acquiring firms' shareholders. One study has calculated that the net results, for shareholders as a class, of all corporate mergers from 1980 to 2001 was an overall *loss* in stock market value of $78 billion.[126] Thus a hyperactive merger market may benefit undiversified shareholders who hold stock only in targets, while destroying value for universal owners.

Why Universal Owners Don't Act Like Universal Owners

Recognizing that "shareholder" is a fictional noun, and that unrelenting pressure to increase stock price can drive corporations to do things that harm the real people who own their shares, naturally raises some difficult questions. In particular, why do so many diversified investors seem blind to their own interests as universal owners? Why do they lobby so hard for individual corporations to do something, anything, to raise share price, even when this harms the value of their other assets and interests?

The answer has to do with structural factors that limit the information available to most individual investors and that create counterproductive incentives for many of the institutional investors that are supposed to represent individual beneficiaries' interests. Consider first the plight of retail investors, typical "mom-and-pop" shareholders. Most have relatively small, diversified investment portfolios, meaning they are likely to hold only very small amounts of stock in any particular corporation. This makes most retail investors rationally apathetic. It simply doesn't make economic sense for them to put much time or effort into finding out what's going on at any of the particular companies in which they hold shares. Instead, they focus their attention on information that is simple, easy, and cheap to obtain: stock price. As a result they usually don't know when a company is externalizing costs onto their other interests. (How many BP shareholders were aware of the risks BP was taking in the Gulf?) They assume a rising share price must translate into a personal benefit, ignorant of the damage being done to other parts of their universal portfolio.

What about institutional investors, especially the mutual funds and pension funds that many individuals rely on to manage their investments for them? Proponents of the universal investor idea, most notably business professors James Hawley and Andrew Williams,[127] have argued that even if individual shareholders are not in a good position to understand or protect their own universal interests, pension funds and mutual funds have the potential to act as stewards for universal owners. After all, because these funds aggregate contributions from many individual beneficiaries, pension and mutual funds control large investment portfolios. The California state pension fund CalPERS, for example, currently manages more than $200 billion in investment assets.[128] This means that a pension or mutual fund may acquire a large enough stake in a particular corporation to overcome rational apathy, and justify spending time and money on acquiring and analyzing the information necessary to understand how that corporation's business strategy affects the value of the stocks, bonds, real estate, bank loans, and other investments in the fund's portfolio. Finally, mutual funds and hedge funds are supposed to act as fiduciaries for their individual beneficiaries. This concept might be read broadly enough to include protecting beneficiaries' interests not only as investors in the fund's portfolio, but also as customers, employees, homeowners, and biological organisms dependent on their environment.

Yet even if pension and mutual funds are better positioned to protect universal investors' interests than retail investors are, they are still unlikely to prove particularly effective stewards for universal investors. First, it is important to recognize that the idea that a pension or mutual fund might protect not only its beneficiaries' financial interests in the fund's portfolio, but also their outside interests in such matters as continued employment, adequate health care, lower taxes, and a clean environment, is—to put it mildly—legally untested. Thus we can expect most mutual and pension fund managers to err on the side of caution and manage their portfolios according to the well-established and accepted fiduciary goal of maximizing the value of the portfolio alone.

Second, the lack of information and rational apathy that makes individual investors poor guardians of their universal portfolios also makes the beneficiaries of pension and mutual funds poor judges of whether their portfolio managers are doing a good job stewarding their universal interests. Just as retail investors default to the cheap, easy strategy of judging corporate performance by whether share price went up or down yesterday, pension and mutual fund beneficiaries judge the performance of fund managers according to whether the value of the fund portfolio went up or down yesterday.

Fund managers accordingly have reason to avoid obvious "rob-Peter-to-pay-Paul" investing strategies that harm the overall value of the portfolios they manage. For example, a fund manager whose portfolio includes both stock in the target and stock in the bidding company in a proposed merger may have a more-jaundiced view of the supposed benefits of the merger than an undiversified shareholder who holds stock in the target alone. But fund managers have little to lose and much to gain from supporting corporate strategies that raise the stock prices of the firms they hold in their portfolios, even when those same strategies harm their beneficiaries' outside interests. We should not be surprised to see a pension fund manager invest in corporations that cut costs by outsourcing jobs to China and India—even if many of the jobs that are outsourced belong to the employees contributing to the pension fund.

How Hedge Funds Harm Universal Owners

If these structural obstacles were not enough, pension and mutual fund managers' ability to act as stewards for universal investors is being challenged today by another powerful force: the rise of hedge funds. Hedge funds are largely unregulated investment pools that are managed by professional traders on behalf of wealthy individuals, foundations, university endowments, and even some pension and mutual funds. They are now estimated to control nearly $2 trillion in investments.[129] And unlike retail investors or pension and mutual funds, hedge funds tend to avoid diversification. Indeed, an activist hedge fund may hold as few as only two or three different securities in its portfolio.

This means that the manager of an undiversified hedge fund—whose human capital also is bound up in his portfolio's performance—comes as close as any living entity can to the Platonic ideal of the undiversified shareholder who cares only about the price of a single company's equity. As a result, hedge fund managers' interests and universal owners' interests often clash. A hedge fund manager will agitate long and hard for business strategies that raise the price of the shares of the few companies he holds, even if other companies' shares suffer as a result. He will pressure companies to accept extreme risks that raise stock price, even if this hurts bond valuations. If he can afford concierge medical care and a private jet, he will happily push for corporations to raise share price by cutting employee health benefits and polluting the environment. (If the beaches on the Gulf of Mexico are soiled by oil, he'll fly to the Bahamas for the weekend.)

Consider, for example, the standard "investing" strategy of activist hedge fund manager Carl Icahn. Icahn is famous for acquiring a substantial position in a particular stock, then using his new shareholder status to demand the company's board put the firm on the auction block and sell it off to the highest bidder (at which point Icahn becomes an ex-shareholder). Among other triumphs, he recently succeeded in pressuring Motorola to sell itself to Google. But on the rare occasion when Icahn has found himself owning stock in a company that wanted to make its own acquisitions—that is, when he is a shareholder in the bidding company that pays a premium, not the target that receives it—he has protested mightily, and worked to block the sale.[130] Clearly, Icahn does not believe the mergers and acquisitions merry-go-round benefits investors as a class. But he is not interested in the wealth of investors as a class. He is interested only in his own wealth.

Why Hedge Funds Have the Advantage over Universal Owners

Undiversified activist hedge funds accordingly pose a special threat to the welfare of universal owners. Of course, an activist hedge fund manager might argue that his interests, and those of his wealthy clients, are just as important and just as worthy of consideration as the interests of more-diversified investors. Similarly, he might argue that even if universal owners are more numerous, this gives them no moral claim to better treatment.

This may be fair enough. Yet even if we treat activist hedge fund and universal investor interests as on a par, the universal owner concept still undermines the case for shareholder primacy. This is because hedge funds' interests not only conflict with those of universal owners: shareholder primacy thinking gives activist hedge funds disproportionate power and influence over corporations.

Activists like Icahn do not suffer from the rational apathy that small retail investors, and even most diversified pension and mutual funds, do. The lack of diversification that puts hedge fund managers' interests at odds with those of most other investors also gives them an enormous advantage when it comes to influencing boards of directors. By taking relatively large positions in relatively few companies, activist hedge funds position themselves to pressure boards with realistic threats of embarrassing news stories and proxy battles if the directors refuse to undertake massive share repurchases, asset sales, employee reductions, and other strategies designed to "unlock shareholder value."

As discussed in Chapter 5, often these hedge fund strategies are nothing more than gimmicks designed to temporarily raise share price without creating lasting wealth. In other cases, schemes to raise share price can be affirmatively destructive to universal investors, destroying value in the other assets in their portfolios. Thus shareholder value thinking becomes especially dangerous to universal investors when hedge funds are added into the mix. Yet many universal investors themselves—retired teachers and firefighters, newlyweds saving to buy a home, parents saving for a child's college tuition—continue to remain largely unaware of the potential for self-destruction implicit in demanding that corporations seek to "maximize shareholder value." In the famed words of the cartoon character Pogo, universal investors have met the enemy, and he is us.

CHAPTER 8

Making Room for Shareholder Conscience

Once we abandon the artifice of viewing investors' interests solely from the perspective of a hypothetical and unrealistic Platonic shareholder, and focus on the reality that human beings who own shares are to at least some degree universal investors, it becomes obvious that conventional shareholder value thinking can be a self-defeating investment strategy for many—if not all—people who happen to own stock. At the same time, the universal investor challenge to shareholder primacy has limits. The category of universal investor is still restricted to those who do in fact hold stocks, whether directly or through a pension or mutual fund.

Compared to the rest of the world, Americans have a great fondness for stock markets. Although stock ownership has declined somewhat in recent years, it is estimated that about 54 percent of Americans hold stocks directly or indirectly.[131] Yet this impressive number still leaves a large number of Americans too poor or too nervous to invest in corporate equities. It also leaves out most of the six billion-plus other people on Earth. It does not include the future generations who will inherit the economy and the planet we leave to them. It does not include animals killed to test cosmetics, endangered species like the spotted owl, or ecologies like the polar ice cap or Amazonian rainforest.

Even if we approach the question of corporate purpose from the perspective of universal owners rather than nonexistent

undiversified "shareholders," we are still focusing only on the
interests of those who belong to the moneyed investing class.
What do these investors want? What serves their interests?

Most People Are Not Psychopaths

Conventional shareholder value thinking presumes that investors, universal or not, care only about their own material
circumstances. Like most of economic theory, it embraces a
homo economicus model of human behavior that presumes
most people are both rational and selfish. But it is increasingly
accepted even among economists that the *homo economicus*
model can be highly inaccurate. This idea provides the basis
for a fourth challenge to the shareholder value paradigm: the
idea of the prosocial shareholder.

One problem with *homo economicus,* observers have pointed out, is that a purely rational and purely selfish person is a
functional psychopath. If "Economic Man" cares nothing for
ethical boundaries or others' welfare, he will lie, cheat, steal,
even murder, whenever it serves his material interests. Not
surprisingly, although *homo economicus* is alive and well in
many economics departments, in recent years a number of
prominent theorists have branched out into so-called behavioral economics, which uses data from psychological experiments to see how real people *really* behave. This experimental
data confirms something both important and reassuring.
Most of us are not conscienceless psychopaths.

The scientific data now demonstrates beyond reasonable
dispute that the vast majority of human beings are at least to
some degree "prosocial." In the right circumstances, most of
us can be counted on to make modest personal sacrifices in
order to follow ethical rules and avoid harming others. (The
estimated 1 percent to 3 percent who cannot be counted on
to do this are indeed psychopaths.) It's easy enough to doubt
pervasive prosociality when reading the daily news. We should

remember, however, that cheating, corruption, rape, and murder make the news because they are relatively rare. (No news-
paper would run the headlines "Large Man Waits Patiently
at Back of Line," or "Employee Doesn't Steal, Even When No
One's Looking.") As the phrase "common decency" suggests,
prosocial behavior is so omnipresent we tend not to notice it.

Nevertheless, the scientific evidence demonstrates that
prosociality is endemic. In one common experiment called a
"social dilemma," for example, anonymous subjects are asked
to choose between a defection strategy that maximizes their
own personal payoffs, and a cooperation strategy in which
they individually receive slightly less but the other members
of the group receive more. As many as 97 percent of subjects
choose to cooperate in some social dilemma games. Similarly,
in another experiment called a "dictator game," subjects are
divided into pairs and one subject is given a sum of money and
asked whether he or she wants to share the money with the
second subject, or not. In some dictator game experiments,
100 percent of the lucky subjects share at least part of their
funds. Not surprisingly, researchers have found that the inci-
dence of such behaviors declines as the personal cost of prosocial action rises: we are more likely to be nice when it only
takes a little, not a lot, of skin off our own noses. Nevertheless,
the evidence overwhelmingly demonstrates that the vast majority of people are willing to make at least small personal
sacrifices to follow their conscience.[132]

Most Shareholders Are Not Psychopaths, Either

There is no reason to think investors are less prosocial than
others. I suspect most Union Carbide shareholders would
have been happy to accept a somewhat lower dividend if this
allowed Union Carbide to adopt safety measures that would
have prevented the deadly explosion in Bhopal, India, that
killed 2,000 and severely injured thousands more. Similarly,

I suspect most Exxon shareholders would have preferred to get slightly lower returns on their investment if this could have prevented the *Exxon Valdez* environmental disaster. In line with these suspicions, one survey has reported that 97 percent of shareholders agree that corporate managers should take some account of nonshareholders' interests in running firms.[133]

Even more direct support for shareholder prosociality can be found in the increasing popularity of socially responsible investment funds ("SRI funds"). SRI funds market themselves to investors by explicitly promising to seek out companies whose practices promote consumer protection, human rights, or environmental sustainability, or to avoid firms that support tobacco, child labor, or weapons production. Although the evidence is mixed, at least some studies suggest that socially responsible investment funds may slightly underperform other funds.[134] Nevertheless, SRI funds have proven highly attractive to investors, taking in investment funds at a much higher rate than the institutional investing industry as a whole. By 2010, 12 percent of all professionally managed assets were managed by socially responsible funds of one sort or another.[135]

Additional evidence of investor prosociality can be found in several states' passage of laws permitting so-called B Corporations, which are required to publicly report their social and environmental performance, and which allow shareholders to sue the B corporation board for failing to adequately pursue the public good. Finally, public corporations and the SEC have for decades wrestled with shareholder proxy proposals demanding that companies act more responsibly by divesting interests in countries with repressive political systems, promoting greater employee diversity, trying to reduce the company's carbon output, and so forth.

But this direct evidence of investor prosociality raises its own problems. Modern science suggests that the vast majority of people are at least to some degree prosocial. Why aren't even more assets invested in socially responsible funds? Why don't more shareholders file proposals asking their companies to reduce their carbon footprints? How can we reconcile the empirical evidence on endemic human prosociality, with most investors' apparent indifference to anything other than stock price?

Obstacles to Investor Prosociality

Harvard law professor Einer Elhauge has explored this puzzle in some detail.[136] He argues persuasively that for at least two reasons, when otherwise prosocial people put on their shareholder hats, they are likely to make asocial investing decisions that cut against their own prosocial inclinations. First, Elhauge points out, diversified shareholders who are uninvolved in and ignorant of a company's day-to-day business decisions are in no position to police against, or even know about, antisocial corporate behavior. To the contrary, because the only thing most investors see is stock price, they are likely to pressure corporate directors and executives to adopt strategies that (unbeknownst to prosocial investors) make corporate harms to third parties more likely. And when disaster strikes, uninvolved shareholders are unlikely to feel personally responsible. How many BP shareholders felt responsible for the *Deepwater Horizon* disaster?

Second, prosocial investors face a classic collective action problem, another investing Tragedy of the Commons. If socially responsible investment funds provide even slightly lower returns than other funds do, the investor who chooses a socially responsible fund incurs a direct personal cost for his prosociality. At the same time, his individual decision to "put his money where his conscience is" is likely to have little or no marginal impact on the behavior of the corporate sector as a whole. Elhauge concludes that "it is remarkable that many people do invest in socially responsible funds considering that their individual decision to do so has no significant impact on furthering even their most altruistic of motives."[137]

Elhauge's argument that the nature of modern stock markets discourages prosocial investing behavior is reinforced by the behavioral data. The scientific evidence reveals that, while most people are capable of and even inclined toward prosociality, our prosocial impulses depend greatly on external social cues. In my 2011 book *Cultivating Conscience: How Good Laws Make Good People*, I label this phenomenon the "Jekyll-Hyde Syndrome."[138] Researchers can dramatically increase the likelihood that experimental subjects will act prosocially by asking them to act prosocially; by leading them to believe other subjects would behave prosocially; and by structuring the experiments so that individuals' prosocial decisions provide larger, rather than smaller, benefits to the other subjects in the group. Conversely, people act more selfishly when told they should be selfish, when they believe others would act selfishly, and when they think their selfishness imposes only a small cost, or no cost, on others.

The result is that most people behave as if they have at least two different personalities. When our Mr. Hyde personality is in charge, we try to maximize our own material welfare without worrying about how our decisions affect others. When prosocial Dr. Jekyll holds the reins, we sacrifice for others and follow legal and ethical moral rules, at least as long as it doesn't cost us too much.[139] The same person who donates money to the Sierra Club and World Wildlife Fund might happily hold stock in oil and timber companies that engage in environmentally destructive drilling and clear-cutting.

Unfortunately, when it comes to investing, shareholder primacy ideology seems almost deliberately designed to bring out our inner Mr. Hydes. The standard shareholder-oriented model of the corporation teaches that it is not only acceptable but morally correct for shareholders to pressure managers to raise share price any way possible, without regard for how the corporation's actions impact stakeholders, society, or the environment. Shareholder value rhetoric also inevitably signals that most other investors are behaving selfishly. Finally, the standard model teaches that selfish investing, far from harming others, actually benefits them by promoting better corporate performance and greater economic efficiency.

Thus we should not be surprised if only a minority of investors chose socially responsible funds. As Elhauge points out, we should be surprised that *any* investors do. The structure of modern stock markets, combined with the rhetoric of shareholder primacy, creates almost insurmountable obstacles to prosocial investing behavior.

Shareholder Value Thinking Reduces Shareholders to Their Lowest Moral Denominator

The unhappy result is that even though most of us are not conscienceless psychopaths, when we make investing decisions *we often act as if we are.* Accordingly, even when corporate executives and directors have perfectly well-tuned moral compasses, shareholder value thinking subjects them to relentless pressure from investors who may act as if they have no moral compass at all. As Einer Elhauge has observed, the situation would be even worse if U.S. corporate law actually required directors to maximize profits: this would "dictate corporate governance by the lowest possible moral denominator . . . enforcing the very soullessness for which corporations have historically been feared."[140]

This observation casts an interesting light on Joel Bakan's influential and award-winning 2004 documentary *The Corporation.* In the film and his accompanying book with the same title, Bakan argued that because corporate managers believe they must maximize shareholder wealth, a corporation is a "psychopathic creature" that "can neither recognize nor act upon moral reasons to refrain from harming others."[141] To the extent this is true, shareholders themselves may be largely to blame. As University of Toronto law professor Ian Lee puts it, "If corporations are in fact 'pathological' profit-maximizers, it is not because of corporate law, but because of pressure from shareholders."[142]

Once again, we see the ideology of shareholder value causing corporations to behave in ways contrary to most shareholders' true interests. Some individual shareholders may in fact be purely self-interested actors—psychopaths—who don't mind if the companies they invest in exploit child labor, deceive consumers, maim employees, or pollute the environment. But the scientific data indicate the vast majority of us would prefer to tolerate at least somewhat diminished returns to avoid such results. Because most studies find that socially responsible investing erodes investors' returns only slightly, if at all,[143] shareholder psychopathy appears to be neither natural nor inevitable but an artifact, the unfortunate outcome of collective action obstacles combined with shareholder value ideology.

CONCLUSION

"Slaves of Some Defunct Economist"

In the 1933 Supreme Court case of *Liggett v. Lee*, Justice Louis Brandeis famously called the public corporation a "Frankenstein monster which states have created by their corporation laws."[144] Brandeis was dissenting in *Liggett*, but his observations about the nature of corporations were right on the mark. In creating the legal institution known as the public corporation, state legislatures breathed life into immensely powerful and long-lived entities that interact with human beings on equal legal footing. The corporate whole is much more than the sum of the biological organisms who act as its directors, executives, and employees. It owns property, accumulates wealth, enters contracts, sues and is sued, campaigns for favorable legislation, and reproduces by forming new corporations. We created corporations; now we share the planet with them. The relationship between our two species can be symbiotic or predatory.

Symbiont or Predator?

So far, humans and corporations seem mostly symbiotic. Just as we tend to overlook human decency and focus on the relatively few cases where people behave badly, we overlook the enormous benefits the corporate form has given the human race. Thanks to corporations, we have cheap and easy access to a host of medical products that prolong and improve our lives: vaccines to prevent disease, antibiotics to cure infections, contraceptives to prevent unwanted pregnancies. Thanks to corporations, we can fly from one coast of the United States to the other in less than six hours and for less than $1,000. (As uncomfortable and expensive as airline travel maybe, it is a vast improvement over making the journey on foot or by covered wagon.) Corporations provide good livelihoods for many individuals, including shareholders who get dividends, bondholders who earn interest, and employees who receive salaries and health and retirement benefits. They benefit our society and future generations by paying taxes, making scientific discoveries, and designing and producing new technologies. They even, as New York University law professor Cynthia Estlund has pointed out, encourage us to treat each other better, promoting gender and racial equality and cooperation in integrated working environments.[145]

Still, there is reason to suspect the American corporate sector is no longer quite as positive an influence on our lives. Over the past decade, public shareholder returns have stagnated; innovation may be declining; corporate employees are increasingly stressed and insecure, or are no longer corporate employees at all. Meanwhile, many of our largest public companies have cast themselves in the role of corporate villain by perpetrating massive frauds (Worldcom, HealthSouth, and Adelphia), spearheading deregulatory lobbying campaigns that brought us to the brink of financial disaster (Enron, Citibank), preying on their customers (Countrywide), creating risks that nearly toppled the financial system (AIG and Goldman Sachs), and damaging the environment (Exxon and BP).

The Role of Shareholder Value Thinking

This book has argued that many of the problems we see in the corporate sector today are the unintended consequences not of corporations as such, but of a mistaken *idea* about corporations: the idea that they ought to be run to maximize shareholder value as measured by share price. Experts increasingly recognize that the conventional shareholder-oriented model of the public corporation isn't the only intellectual game in town. Indeed, the model doesn't fit reality. Shareholder primacy is not required by the law; the theory underpinning it mischaracterizes the corporation's true economic structure; it is not supported by the empirical evidence on corporate performance. Perhaps most disturbing, far from having proven itself a governance cure, the increasing influence of shareholder value thinking on business law and practice has been accompanied by, if anything, a decline in American corporate and economic performance.

Nevertheless, shareholder value thinking continues to wield enormous influence in the business world and in the popular press. Worse, it still dominates instruction in law and business classes. A recent Brookings study of the curricula of top law and business schools concluded that "many professional school courses emphasize maximizing corporate profits and shareholder value" and that "the emphasis on shareholder value is especially prevalent in law schools." As a result, "students believe the primary purpose of the corporation is to maximize shareholder value, and they believe this is how current corporate leaders behave when they are making decisions."[146]

Why does shareholder value thinking have such staying power? As already noted, the shareholder primacy approach appeals to some influential interests. These include educators and journalists looking for a sound-bite explanation of corporations to offer their students and readers; researchers seeking an easy way to measure corporate performance; activist hedge fund managers hoping for intellectual cover as they agitate for personally profitable but socially costly business strategies; and CEOs delighted to discover that the mantra of "increase shareholder wealth" gives them room to increase their own wealth through stock options and other pay-for-performance schemes.

But the needs of interest groups only partly explain how, after decades of managerialist thinking, shareholder primacy came to dominate modern discussions of corporate purpose. After all, as we saw in Part II, shareholder value ideology often harms the interests of another powerful interest group: investors themselves. Nevertheless, many investors—including not only mom-and-pop individual investors, but also institutions like pension and mutual funds, not to mention activist hedge funds—were at the front of the line in demanding that corporations de-stagger their boards, use stock options and other share-price-based schemes to compensate executives, and adopt majority rather than plurality voting rules to make it harder for incumbent directors to seek reelection. Similarly, investors have supported SEC initiatives to promote "shareholder democracy" by eliminating broker voting, giving shareholders access to corporate funds to mount proxy battles, and adopting other rule changes intellectually grounded in shareholder value thinking. Shareholders are among the most ardent supporters of shareholder primacy, even as they are its victims.

The Lure of Mythology

In his 2007 bestseller *The Black Swan*, author and former hedge fund manager Nassim Taleb offers an explanation for why shareholder value mythology has proven so powerful. According to Taleb, "A novel, a story, a myth, or a tale, all have the same function: they spare us from the complexity of the world and shield us from its randomness."[147] The greatest appeal of the shareholder value myth may lie in how it seems to tame and simplify an unruly and complex reality: the natures of shareholders themselves.

This book has shown that the idea of maximizing share-holder value rests on an impossible abstraction of "the share-holder" as a Platonic entity that cares only about the market price of a single corporation's equity. This means that share-holder value is an inherently flawed concept, because in reality different shareholders have different values. Contemporary experts in corporate law and economics increasingly recognize that shareholders are human beings with differing investment time frames, different interests ex ante and ex post, different degrees of diversification, and different attitudes toward sacrificing personal wealth to follow ethical rules and avoid harming others. Conventional shareholder value thinking reconciles different shareholders' conflicting desires by simply assuming the conflicts away.

In the process, shareholder value ideology reduces investors to their lowest possible common human denominator. It favors the desires of the pathologically impatient investor over the long-sighted; favors the opportunistic and untrustworthy over those who want to be able to keep ex ante commitments to stakeholders and each other; favors the irrationally self-destructive over those more sensitive to their own interests as diversified universal owners; and favors the psychopathically selfish over the prosocial concerned about other people, future generations, and the planet. This single-dimensioned conception of shareholder interest is not only unrealistic, but dysfunctional.

We Don't Need a Single Metric

Some experts might argue we have no alternative. One common defense of using shareholder value as the sole criterion for judging corporate performance rests on the claim that unless we have a single, objective measure to judge how well directors and executives are running firms, these corporate agents will run amok. As economist Michael Jensen has put the argument, "Any organization must have a single-valued objective as a precursor to purposeful or rational behavior. . . . It is logically impossible to maximize in more than one dimension at the same time . . . Thus, telling a manager to maximize current profits, market share, future growth profits, and anything else one pleases will leave that manager with no way to make a reasoned decision. In effect it leaves the manager with no objective."[148] According to Jensen, "[t]he solution is to define a true (single dimensional) score for measuring performance for the organization."[149]

This perspective ignores the obvious human capacity to balance, albeit imperfectly, competing interests and responsibilities. Every day, parents with more than one child must balance the interests of competing siblings (not to mention balancing their children's welfare against their own). Judges routinely balance justice against judicial efficiency. Teachers balance the interests of students who are quick against those who are slow, professors balance teaching demands against research and scholarship, shopkeepers balance the hope of making one more sale against the desire to get home in time for the family dinner. This is not to say balancing interests is easy. But the fact that it can be hard doesn't mean it can't be done. It is done every day. Balancing interests—decently satisfying several sometimes-competing objectives, rather than trying to "maximize" only one—is the rule and not the exception in human affairs.

A second, related argument is that even if the conventional principal-agent model of the corporation is flawed, it is the only model that reliably tells us what corporations should do. Alternative theories of corporate purpose—for example, stakeholder welfare theories, or team production theories— are controversial, and perhaps more important, don't always give clear guidance in particular cases on what, exactly, directors and managers should adopt as the company's goal. If you only have one tool at hand, the argument goes, that is the tool that you must use.

This argument overlooks the possibility that, sometimes, a tool can be so obviously inappropriate and ill-suited to a particular task that we are better off leaving it to gather dust in the toolbox. Suppose you are a doctor trying to help a patient with a stomachache, and your only tool is a chainsaw. By blithely picking up the chainsaw and setting to work, you would make matters much worse than they already are.

Similarly, when we insist on gauging the performance of the American corporate sector solely by the share price performance of individual companies, we are ignoring the diverse interests and values of different shareholders to focus only on those of a very narrow subset that is particularly short-sighted, opportunistic, indifferent to external costs, and lacking in conscience. Collectively, we might do far better if we are willing to tolerate some ambiguity about what the ultimate purpose of the corporate entity should be. As former Delaware Chancellor William T. Allen has put it, "It is perhaps too much to expect us, as a people—or our law—to have a single view of the purpose of an institution so large, pervasive and important as our public corporations. These entities are too important to generate that sort of agreement."[150]

Paying Attention to Reality

Abandoning the quixotic and ultimately self-defeating idea that corporate success and corporate purpose can and should be measured by a single objective metric allows us to understand a host of otherwise-puzzling realities of corporate law and practice. Perhaps the most obvious is how public corporations managed to develop and thrive in the first place, despite the awkward fact that they are controlled not by shareholders or bondholders but by boards of directors empowered to employ corporate assets toward almost any lawful end. Thanks to dispersed shareholders' rational apathy and the business judgment rule, for most of the twentieth century directors of public companies who did not breach their loyalty duties enjoyed virtually unfettered discretion to set corporate policy, even over shareholders' vocal objections. This without doubt increased "agency costs," and often left directors with less than crystal-clear guidance on their ultimate goal. It did not, however, stop American public corporations from producing excellent results for investors as well as for employees, consumers, and communities.

More recently, as shareholder value thinking has gained traction and boards have become more attuned to shareholder demands, investor returns have, if anything, declined instead of improving. Meanwhile, truly public companies are disappearing. Many firms are going private, fewer are going public, and large numbers of the companies that do go public (Google, LinkedIn, Zynga) are adopting dual-class voting structures that disenfranchise public investors. This suggests that shareholder primacy may work fine as long as the shareholder in question is an individual or small group, and the corporation essentially a closely held company. But the disappearance of the classic U.S. public corporation provides indirect evidence that shareholder primacy is not an attractive or effective business model for companies with dispersed public shareholders.

Some Lessons from the New Thinking

That possibility offers a host of important lessons for corporate managers, policymakers, and investors themselves. Turning first to the managers who run corporations, the new work on corporate purpose teaches that directors and executives do a disservice to their firms and their investors if they use share price as their only guiding star. To build enduring value, managers must focus on the long term as well as tomorrow's stock quotes, and must sometimes make credible if informal commitments to customers, suppliers, employees, and other stakeholders whose specific investments contribute to the firm's success. Moreover, emphasizing share price can harm shareholders' other economic and personal interests, including the prosocial interests of shareholders willing to sacrifice some profits in return for greater corporate social responsibility.

Thus, if executives and especially boards of directors want to truly promote "shareholder value," they need to embrace the discretion that corporate law grants them to use their power and authority over the firm as a means to address (as Iman Anabtawi puts it) "the need for mediating the various and often conflicting interests of shareholders themselves."[151] We should not expect boards to do a perfect job of mediating these "various and often conflicting" shareholder interests. However, there is no reason to think boards can't mediate well enough that shareholder interest-balancing by a board is preferable to a board that slavishly responds only to the concerns of the most short-sighted, opportunistic, undiversified, and unethical subset of shareholders. In this vein, boards should keep in mind that balancing becomes especially difficult if the heavy weight of self-interest is added to one side of the scale. Stock options and other compensation schemes that tie executive or director pay primarily to share price undermine corporate managers' motivation to pursue more authentic visions of shareholder value.

Second, if we want to keep public corporations as a vibrant force in the America economy, policymakers and would-be reformers need to stop reflexively responding to every business crisis or scandal du jour by trying to "improve" corporate governance by making boards and executives more "accountable" to certain shareholders' demands. For over two decades, the Congress, the SEC, and a variety of private "policy entrepreneurs" have successfully pushed through a number of individually modest but collectively significant corporate regulations designed to make managers more focused on shareholders and shareholder wealth. Examples include the SEC's 1992 proxy rule changes making it easier for institutional investors to coordinate their corporate lobbying efforts; the 1993 tax code changes encouraging public companies to tie executive pay to objective performance metrics like stock price; the SEC's 2002 rule requiring mutual funds to publicly disclose how they vote the shares held in their portfolios (which discourages funds from habitually voting with management); certain provisions of the 2002 Sarbanes-Oxley Act that require audit committees of public companies to be comprised entirely of independent directors; and the SEC's 2010 elimination of broker voting of customer shares (brokers, too, routinely voted with management). These "reforms" have failed to raise either investor returns or shareholder satisfaction. There is no reason to think that continuing to promote "shareholder democracy" through even more rules, like the SEC's controversial proxy access proposal, will do a better job of serving shareholders' collective welfare. To the contrary, while such supposedly shareholder-friendly regulations may provide an immediate windfall to certain types of shareholders (especially undiversified hedge funds that hold shares for only a year or two), they may ultimately work against the interests of most shareholders as a class.

Third and relatedly, investors themselves—including not only individual retail investors, but especially institutional investors like mutual and pension funds that are supposed to ultimately serve the interests of their individual beneficiaries—need to rethink the common assumption that anything that raises the share price of a particular company at a particular time necessarily serves investor welfare. Conventional shareholder primacy implicitly assumes that a share price increase necessarily means a commensurate increase in investor well-being. The new scholarship on the nature and purpose of the corporation logically severs this supposed linkage. Proposals to promote greater "shareholder democracy" or to "incentivize" executives by tying their pay to stock price can attract strong political support from vocal minority shareholder groups, like hedge funds, that hope to reap windfall gains by temporarily increasing the share price of particular companies at particular times. But there is reason to suspect such strategies ultimately hurt the "investing class" as a whole.

Ideas about Corporations Matter

The time has come to liberate ourselves from the tyranny of shareholder value thinking. In the interest of maximizing shareholder value, corporate directors have de-staggered their boards, adopted share-based executive compensation schemes, and cut back on research and development and employee benefits in order to meet quarterly earnings estimates. In the interest of shareholder value, pension and mutual funds, and even individual investors, have joined with hedge funds to pressure boards to "unlock value" through repurchases and asset sales, while turning a blind eye to questions of corporate responsibility and ethics. Regulatory changes have played a role in moving Corporate America closer to the standard shareholder-oriented model, but the most important factor has been the business world's own intellectual embrace of shareholder primacy ideology. Investors and managers alike have come to accept shareholder value thinking as the necessary, if sometimes unattractive, foundation of the business world.

John Maynard Keynes famously said that "the ideas of economists and political philosophers, both when they are right and when they are wrong, are more powerful than is commonly understood. Indeed the world is ruled by little else. Practical men, who believe themselves to be quite exempt from any intellectual influence, are usually the slaves of some defunct economist." Viewed dispassionately, shareholder value ideology shows all the signs of a defunct economist's idea. It is inconsistent with American corporate law; misstates the economic structure of public companies; and lacks persuasive empirical support. Not only does shareholder value ideology fail on inductive grounds, it is riddled with deductive flaws as well, especially its premise that the only shareholder whose values should count is the shareholder who is myopic, untrustworthy, self-destructive, and without a social conscience.

Nevertheless, as described in the recent Brookings report, shareholder primacy is such a seductively simple idea that it continues to be taught in law schools, business schools, and economics departments. This is disturbing because, as the report's author observes, "If schools emphasize a particular set of values or approaches, it will reverberate for decades to come. These values will determine how business leaders and lawyers behave, professional association standards are set, and policies are adopted."[152]

The good news is that among experts, shareholder value dogma shows signs of being in decline. To return to Thomas Kuhn, the shareholder primacy paradigm is failing, and alternative paradigms are rising to take its place. This book has explored a suite of new, more nuanced theories of corporate purpose and shareholder interest. These alternatives share a common theme: they all sever the supposed linkage between "shareholder value" and shareholder welfare by showing how different shareholders have different interests and values. They also all suggest how giving managers discretion to balance among different shareholders' competing interests can ultimately serve the interests of investors as a class, over time, better than a strict shareholder primacy rule would.

In the process, the new thinking on shareholder value also goes a long way toward resolving, at least in a practical sense, the century-long Great Debate on the purpose of public corporations. Conventional shareholder primacy stands on the brink of intellectual failure. To survive it must evolve into a new, more complex, and more subtle understanding of what shareholders really want from corporations. This understanding acknowledges that it may be impossible to define the "purpose" of the corporation in terms of a single, easily measured goal, and that the objective of any particular corporation may be best determined not by regulators, judges, or professors, or even by any individual shareholder or group of shareholders, but by a board of directors. That board is charged with serving the best interests of (as case law puts it) "the corporation and its shareholders"—including long-term shareholders, shareholders eager to make ex ante commitments to stakeholders, diversified shareholders, and prosocial shareholders. Expanding our understanding of the nature of "the shareholder" this way benefits not just investors, but the rest of us as well.

Notes

Notes to the Introduction

[1] National Commission on the BP *Deepwater Horizon* Oil Spill and Offshore Drilling, *Deep Water: The Gulf Oil Disaster and the Future of Offshore Drilling* (January 2011).

[2] *Id.*, 2.

[3] *Id.*, 218.

[4] Henry Hansmann and Reinier Kraakman, "The End of History for Corporate Law," 89 *Georgetown Law Review* 439 (2001).

[5] David Weild and Edward Kim, "A Wake-Up Call for America," Grant Thornton Capital Market Series 1 (November 2009).

[6] John Kao, *Innovation Nation: How America is Losing Its Innovation Edge, Why It Matters, and What We Can Do to Get It Back* (New York: Free Press 2007). A study by the Information Technology and Innovations Foundations recently concluded that in a study of 40 developed and developing nations from 1999 and 2009, "The United States has made the least progress of the 40 nations/regions in improvement in international competitiveness and innovation over the last decade." Robert D. Atkinson & Scott Andes, *The Atlantic Century: Benchmarking EU & U.S. Innovation and Competitiveness* (February 2009).

[7] National Commission, *Deep Water*, 229.

[8] Francesco Guerrera, "Welch Condemns Share Price Focus," *Financial Times* (March 12, 2009), www.ft.com /intl/cms/s/0/294ff1f2-0f27-11de-ba10-0000779fd2ac. html#axzz1eHkdklrf.

[9] Iman Anabtawi, "Some Skepticism About Increasing Shareholder Power," 53 *University of California Los Angeles Law Review* 561, 564 (2006).

[10] "Capitalism's Waning Popularity: Market of Ideas: A Global Poll Shows an Ideology in Apparent Decline," *Economist* 70 (April 9, 2011).

Notes to Chapter One

[11] Adolf Berle and Gardiner Means, *The Modern Corporation and Private Property* (New Brunswick, U.S.A. and London: Transaction Publishers, 1991, originally published 1932).

[12] William W. Bratton and Michael L. Wachter, "Shareholder Primacy's Corporatist Origins: Adolf Berle and 'The Modern Corporation,'" 34 *Journal of Corporation Law* 99, 100–103 (2008).

[13] William T. Allen, Jack B. Jacobs and Leo E. Strine, Jr., "The Great Takeover Debate: A Meditation on Bridging the Conceptual Divide," 69 *University of Chicago Law Review* 1067 (2002).

[14] Berle and Means, *The Modern Corporation*.

[15] Adolf A. Berle, "Corporate Powers as Powers in Trust," 44 *Harvard Law Review* 1049 (1931).

[16] E. Merrick Dodd, "For Whom Are Corporate Managers Trustees?" 45 *Harvard Law Review* 1148 (1932).

[17] Adolf A. Berle, *The 20th Century Capitalist Revolution* (New York: Harcourt, Brace, 1954), 169.

[18] Milton Friedman, "The Social Responsibility of Business is to Increase Its Profits," *New York Times Magazine* 32 (September 13, 1970).

[19] Michael C. Jensen and William H. Meckling, "Theory of the Firm: Managerial Behavior, Agency Costs and Ownership Structure," Vol. 3, No. 4 *Journal of Financial Economics* 305 (October, 1976).

[20] Steven M. Teles, *The Rise of the Conservative Legal Movement: The Battle for Control of the Law* (Princeton, New Jersey and Oxford: Princeton University Press, 2008) 216.

[21] Brian J. Hall, "Six Challenges in Designing Equity-Based Pay," 15 Accenture Journal of Applied Corporate Finance (2003) 23, cited in Jill E. Fisch, "Measuring Efficiency in Corporate Law: The Role of Shareholder Primacy," 31 *Journal of Corporation Law* 639 n.5 (Spring 2006).

[22] Lucian Bebchuk and Jesse M. Fried, *Pay without Performance: The Unfulfilled Promise of Executive Compensation* (Cambridge, Massachusetts: Harvard University Press, 2006).

[23] Jeffrey N. Gordon, "The Rise of Independent Directors in the United States, 1950–2005: Of Shareholder Value and Stock Market Prices," 59 *Stanford Law Review* 1529, 1530 (2007).

[24] Henry Hansmann and Reinier Kraakman, "The End of History for Corporate Law," 89 *Georgetown Law Review* 439 (2001).

[25] Hansmann and Kraakman, "The End of History," 440–441.

[26] Id., 468.

[27] Margaret M. Blair, "Post Enron Assessments of Comparative Corporate Governance" (2002), http://papers.ssrn.com/sol3/papers.cfm?abstract_id=316663.

Notes to Chapter Two

[28] Tina Rosenberg, "A Scorecard for Companies with a Conscience," *New York Times* (April 4, 2011), http://opinionator.blogs.nytimes.com/2011/04/11/a-scorecard-for-companies-with-a-conscience. Similarly, *Times* columnist Joe Nocera defended GE's ruthless exploitation of corporate tax loopholes on the grounds that "the executives who run America's corporations have a fiduciary duty to maximize profit for their shareholders." Joe Nocera, "Who Could Blame GE?" *New York Times* (April 4, 2011), www.nytimes.com/2011/04/05/opinion/05nocera.html.

[29] Marjorie Kelly, *The Divine Right of Capital: Dethroning the Corporate Aristocracy* (San Francisco: Berrett-Koehler Publishers, 2001, 2003), 54.

[30] Joel Bakan, *The Corporation: The Pathological Pursuit of Profit and Power* (New York, London, Toronto, Sydney: Free Press, 2004).

[31] *Dodge v. Ford Motor Co.*, 170 N.W. 668 (Mich. 1919).

[32] Einer Elhauge, "Sacrificing Corporate Profits in the Public Interest," 80 *New York University Law Review* 733, 772–75 (2005).

[33] Id., 684.

[34] For examples, see Stephen M. Bainbridge, "Director Primacy: The Means and Ends of Corporate Governance," 97 *Northwestern University Law Review* 547, 574–75 (2003); Joel Bakan, *The Corporation* 36; Marjorie Kelly, *The Divine Right of Capital* 52–53.

[35] *Blackwell v. Nixon*, Civ. A. No. 9041, 1991 WL 194725, at *4 (Del. Ch. Sept. 26, 1991).

[36] The federal Circuit Court for the District of Columbia recently struck down an SEC attempt to impose a "proxy access" requirement that public corporations give certain share-

holders access to company funds to solicit proxies. *Business Roundtable et al. v. Securities and Exchange Commission,* No. 10-1305 (D.C. Cir., July 22, 2011).

[37] Delaware General Corporation Law, Section 102 (2011).

[38] Lynn A. Stout, "Why We Should Stop Teaching *Dodge v. Ford,*" 3 *Virginia Law & Business Review* 163 (2008).

[39] Delaware General Corporation Law, Section 101 (2011).

[40] Stout, "Why We Should Stop Teaching," 169.

[41] Id.

[42] Id., 170.

[43] Margaret M. Blair and Lynn A. Stout, "A Team Production Theory of Corporate Law," 85 *Virginia Law Review* 247, 293 (1999).

[44] *Unocal Corp. v. Mesa Petroleum Co.,* 493 A.2d 946 (1985).

[45] *Shlensky v. Wrigley,* 95 Ill. App.2d 173, 237 N.E.2d 776 (1968).

[46] *Air Products and Chemicals, Inc. v. Airgas Inc.,* Civ. 5249-CC, 5256-CC (Del. Ch., Feb. 15, 2011) 92, citing *Paramount Communications Inc. v. Time, Inc.,* 571 A.2d 1140, 1150 (Del. 1990).

[47] *Revlon, Inc. v. MacAndrews & Forbes Holdings, Inc.,* 506 A.2d 173 (Del. 1986).

[48] Lynn A. Stout, "Why We Should Stop Teaching *Dodge v. Ford,*" 3 *Virginia Law & Business Review,* 163, 171-172 (2008).

Notes to Chapter Three

[49] William T. Allen, Jack B. Jacobs and Leo E. Strine, Jr., "The Great Takeover Debate: A Mediation on Bridging the Conceptual Divide," 69 *University of Chicago Law Review* 1067 (2002); Margaret M. Blair and Lynn A. Stout, "A Team Production Theory of Corporate Law," 85 *Virginia Law Review* 247 (1999); Einer Elhauge, "Sacrificing Corporate Profits in the Public Interest," 80 *New York University Law Review* 733 (2005); D. Gordon Smith, "The Shareholder Primacy Norm," 23 *Journal of Corporation Law* 277 (1998).

[50] Henry Hansmann and Reinier Kraakman, "The End of History for Corporate Law," 89 *Georgetown Law Review* 439 (2001).

[51] For a classic example, see Lucian Bebchuk and Jesse M. Fried, *Pay without Performance: The Unfulfilled Promise of Executive Compensation* (Cambridge, Massachusetts: Harvard University Press, 2006).

52 Martin Lipton and Paul K. Rowe critique this view in "Pills, Polls, and Professors: A Reply to Professor Gilson," 27 *Delaware Journal of Corporate Law* 1 (2002).

53 A recent SEC attempt to impose just such a "proxy access" rule on public companies was struck down by a federal court. *Business Roundtable et al. v. Securities and Exchange Commission*, No. 10–1305 at 12 (D.C. Cir., July 22, 2011).

54 Milton Friedman also expressed this view still earlier in his bestseller *Capitalism and Freedom* (Chicago, Illinois: University of Chicago Press, 1962).

55 Roger Martin, *Fixing the Game: Bubbles, Crashes, and What Capitalism Can Learn from the NFL* (Boston, Massachusetts: Harvard Business Review Press, 2011), 11.

56 Richard A. Posner and Kenneth E. Scott, *The Economics of Corporation Law and Securities Regulation* (Boston and Toronto: Little, Brown and Company, 1980), 39–56.

57 Frank H. Easterbrook and Daniel R. Fischel, *The Economic Structure of Corporate Law* (Cambridge, Massachusetts and London: Harvard University Press, 1991).

58 Hansmann and Kraakman, "The End of History," 468.

59 Fischer Black and Myron Scholes, "The Pricing of Options and Corporate Liabilities," 81 *Journal of Political Economy* 637 (1973).

60 Easterbrook and Fischel, *The Economic Structure of Corporate Law*, 36–37.

61 Lynn M. LoPucki, "The Myth of the Residual Owner: An Empirical Study," *Washington University Law Quarterly* 1341, 1343 (2004).

62 Lynn A. Stout, "Bad and Not-So-Bad Arguments for Shareholder Primacy," 75 *Southern California Law Review* 1192–95 (2002).

63 Delaware General Corporation Law, Section 170 (2011).

64 Id.

65 Delaware General Corporation Law, Sections 108, 170 (2011).

66 American Law Institute, Restatement (3d) of Agency, Section 1.01 (2006).

67 Delaware General Corporation Law, Section 141 (2011).

68 Robert Charles Clark, Corporate Law (Boston and Toronto: Little Brown, 1986), 95.

[69] Margaret M. Blair and Lynn A. Stout, "A Team Production Theory of Corporate Law," 85 *Virginia Law Review* 247, 303 (1999).

[70] Lynn A. Stout, "Bad and Not-So-Bad Arguments for Shareholder Primacy," 75 Southern California Law Review 1189, 1203–124 (2002).

[71] Hansmann and Kraakman, "End of History," 443 (emphasis added).

[72] Frank H. Easterbrook and Daniel R. Fischel, *The Economic Structure of Corporate Law* (Cambridge, Massachusetts and London: Harvard University Press, 1991), 38.

[73] Mark J. Roe, "The Shareholder Wealth Maximization Norm and Industrial Organizations," 149 *University of Pennsylvania Law Review* 2063, 2065 (2001).

Notes to Chapter Four

[74] Renee Adams and Daniel Ferreira, "One Share-One Vote: The Empirical Evidence," 12 *Review of Finance* 51 (2008).

[75] Valentin Dimitriv and Prem C. Jain, "Recapitalization of One Class of Common Stock into Dual-Class: Growth and Long-Run Stock Returns," 12 *Journal of Corporate Finance* 342 (2006).

[76] Sanjay Bhagat and Bernard S. Black, "Independent Directors" (2008), http://papers.ssrn.com/sol3/papers.cfm?abstract_id=1139191.

[77] Sanjay Bhagat and Richard H. Jefferis, *The Econometrics of Corporate Governance Studies* (Cambridge and London: MIT Press, 2002); Lawrence Brown and Marcus Caylor "Corporate Governance and Firm Operating Performance," 32 *Review of Quantitative Finance and Accounting* 129 (2009).

[78] Id.

[79] "Schumpeter: Corporate Constitutions: The World Knows Less about What Makes for Good Corporate Governance Than It Likes to Think, *Economist* 74 (October 30, 2010), www.economist.com/node/17359354.

[80] See, e.g., Dan R. Dalton, et al., "The Fundamental Agency Problem and Its Mitigation," 1 *Academy of Management Annals* 1–64 (December 2007).

81 Roberta Romano, "The Sarbanes Oxley Act and the Makings of Quack Corporate Governance," 114 *Yale Law Journal* 114 (2005).

82 Sanjai Bhagat, Brian Bolton and Roberta Romano, "The Promise and Peril of Corporate Governance Indices," 108 *Columbia Law Review* 1814 (2008).

83 *Business Roundtable et al. v. Securities and Exchange Commission*, No. 10–1305 at 12 (D.C. Cir., July 22, 2011).

84 For example, one recent study of hedge funds concluded that "hedge funds are not short-term in focus" because they had a median holding period of 12 to 20 months. Alon Brav, et al., "Hedge Fund Activism, Corporate Governance, and Firm Performance," Vol. 63, No. 4 *Journal of Finance* 1731 (2008).

85 Margaret M. Blair, "Shareholder Value, Corporate Governance, and Corporate Performance: A Post-Enron Reassessment of the Conventional Wisdom," 61 (2003), http://papers.ssrn .com/sol3/papers.cfm?abstract_id=334240.

86 Jeffrey N. Gordon, "The Rise of Independent Directors in the United States, 1950–2005: Of Shareholder Value and Stock Market Prices," 59 *Stanford Law Review* 1529, 1530 (2007).

87 Roger Martin, *Fixing the Game: Bubbles, Crashes, and What Capitalism Can Learn from the NFL* (Boston, Massachusetts: Harvard Business Review Press, 2011), 63.

88 Citibank lobbying played a central role in the 1999 passage of the Gramm-Leach-Bliley Act, which lifted banking restrictions and has been cited as a cause of the 2008 crisis. Financial Crisis Inquiry Commission, *Final Report of the National Commission on the Causes of the Financial and Economic Crisis in the United States* (New York: Public Affairs, 2011), 55. Similarly, Enron lobbied for the passage of the 2000 Commodity Futures Modernization Act, which deregulated deriviatives markets and has also been cited as a cause of the crisis. See Lynn A. Stout, "Derivatives and the Legal Origin of the 2008 Credit Crisis," 1 *Harvard Business Law Review* 1, 26 (2011).

89 David Weild and Edward Kim, "A Wake-Up Call for America," Grant Thornton Capital Market Series 1–2 (November 2009).

90 John C. Coates, "Explaining Variation in Takeover Defenses: Blame the Lawyers," 89 *California Law Review* 1301, 1397 (2001).

[91] Jennifer G. Hill, "Then and Now: Professor Berle and the Unpredictable Shareholder," 33 *Seattle University Law Review* 1017 (2010).

[92] Where only about 20 percent of U.S. public corporations pay regular dividends, more than half of U.K. firms do. Stephen P. Ferris, Nilanjan Sen, and Ho Pei Yui, "God Save the Queen and Her Dividends," 79 *Journal of Business* 1149–1150 (2006).

[93] For a survey of efficient market theory, see Lynn A. Stout, "The Mechanisms of Market Efficiency: An Introduction to the New Finance," 23 *Journal of Corporation Law* 635 (2003).

Notes to Chapter Five

[94] For a survey of efficient market theory, see Lynn A. Stout, "The Mechanisms of Market Efficiency: An Introduction to the New Finance," 23 *Journal of Corporation Law* 635 (2003).

[95] Id.

[96] John Quiggen, *Zombie Economics: How Dead Ideas Still Walk among Us* (Princeton, New Jersey and London: Princeton University Press (2010).

[97] Fischer Black, "Noise," 41 *Journal of Finance* 533 (1986).

[98] William W. Bratton, "Hedge Funds and Governance Targets," 95 *Georgetown Law Review* 1375, 1410 (2007).

[99] Leo E. Strine, Jr., "One Fundamental Corporate Governance Question We Face: Can Corporations Be Managed for the Long Term Unless Their Powerful Electorates Also Act and Think Long Term?," 66 *Business Law* 1, 11 (2010).

[100] According to the Federal Reserve, about 36 percent of corporate equities are held by households, 25 percent by mutual funds, and 17 percent by private and government pension funds. Federal Reserve Statistical Release, Flow of Funds Accounts, www.federalreserve.gov/releases/z1/Current/z1r-4.pdf (June 9, 2011) 92, Table L.213.

[101] Aspen Institute Business and Society Program, *Overcoming Short-Termism: A Call for a More Responsible Approach to Investment and Business Management* (September 9, 2009), www.aspeninstitute.org/publications/overcoming-short-termism-call-more-responsible-approach-investment-business-management.

[102] John C. Bogle, "Reflections on the Evolution of Mutual Fund Governance," Vol. 1, No. 1 *Journal of Business & Technology Law* 47 (2006).

[103] Stout, "Mechanisms," 651–69.

[104] John R. Graham, Cam Harvey, and Shiva Rajgopal, "Value Destruction and Financial Reporting Decisions," 62 *Financial Analysts Journal* 27–39 (2006).

[105] Stout, "Mechanisms," 647–48.

[106] Bratton, "Hedge Funds," 1401.

[107] Martin Lipton, "Takeover Bids in the Target's Boardroom," 35 *Business Lawyer* 104 (1979)(emphasis deleted).

[108] For example, ISS routinely recommends that corporations de-stagger their boards to make hostile takeovers easier and historically supported pay-for-performance schemes linking executive compensation to share price.

[109] Roger Martin, *Fixing the Game: Bubbles, Crashes, and What Capitalism Can Learn from the NFL* (Boston, Massachusetts: Harvard Business Review Press, 2011), 12–13.

[110] Id., 21, 23.

[111] Id., 193.

[112] Gena Chon et al., "Activists Pressed for Kraft Spinoff," *Wall Street Journal* (August 5, 2011), http://online.wsj.com/article/SB10001424053111903454504576487720348267828.html.

[113] Bratton, "Hedge Funds," 1410, 1419.

Notes to Chapter Six

[114] Harold Demsetz, *The Economics of the Business Firm: Seven Critical Commentaries* (Cambridge: Cambridge University Press, 1995), 50.

[115] Demsetz, *The Economics of the Business Firm*, 51.

[116] Margaret M. Blair, "Locking In Capital: What Corporate Law Achieved for Business Organizers in the Nineteenth Century," 51 *UCLA Law Review* 404 (2003).

[117] Henry Hansmann and Reinier Kraakman, "The Essential Role of Organizational Law," 110 *Yale Law Journal* 404 (2000).

[118] Margaret M. Blair and Lynn A. Stout, "A Team Production Theory of Corporate Law," 85 *Virginia Law Review* 247, 303 (1999).

[119] Mutual funds are more likely to support dismantling takeover defenses in the firms they own, than other shareholders are.

"ICI Defends Mutual Fund Voting Record," Vol. 8, No. 10 *Investor Relations* 15 (October 2008).

[120] Andrei Shleifer and Lawrence H. Summers, "Breach of Trust in Hostile Takeovers," in *Corporate Takeovers: Causes and Consequences* (Alan J. Auerbach ed.) (Chicago and London: University of Chicago Press, 1988), 35, 49–50.

[121] Henrick Cronqvist, et al., "Do Entrenched Managers Pay Their Workers More?" 64 *Journal of Finance* 309 (2009); Andrew Von Nordenflycht, "The Public Corporation—Friend of Foe of Professional Ethics? Ownership and Ethics in Securities Brokerage," http://papers.ssrn.com/sol3/papers.cfm?abstract_id=1819339 (April 22, 2011).

[122] MetLife, *9th Annual Study of Employee Benefits Trends* 3, 9, 15 (2011), www.metlife.com/business/insights-and-tools/industry-knowledge/employee-benefits-trends-study/index.html.

[123] Six of the ten largest U.K. companies are in finance or commodities extraction. "Top Ten Most Valuable Companies in the FTSE 100: In Pictures," *The Telegraph* (March 10, 2011), www.telegraph.co.uk/finance/markets/8371481/Top-ten-most-valuable-companies-in-the-FTSE-100-in-pictures.html.

[124] Mark Atherton, "BP—Is Your Pension Safe?," *Sunday Times* (June 11, 2010), www.timesonline.co.uk/tol/money/pensions/article7148161.ece.

Notes to Chapter Seven

[125] William W. Bratton, "Hedge Funds and Governance Targets," 95 *Georgetown Law Review* 1375, 1425 (2007).

[126] Id.

[127] James P. Hawley & Andrew T. Williams, *The Rise of Fiduciary Capitalism: How Institutional Investors Can Make Corporate America More Democratic*, (Philadelphia: University of Pennsylvania Press, 2000).

[128] In November 2011, CalPERS reported $236 billion in assets under management as of August 31, 2011. www.calpers.ca.gov/eip-docs/about/facts/investments.pdfr.

129 Matteo Tonello, "Hedge Fund Activism: Findings and Recommendations for Corporations and Investors," Conference Board Research Report R-1434–08, 11 (2008).

130 Bratton, "Hedge Funds," 1377–1378. Another study of activist funds concluded generally that "as shareholders of the potential acquirer, hedge funds have tried to prevent the consummation of the transaction." Marcel Kahan and Edward B. Rock, "Hedge Funds in Corporate Governance," 155 *University of Pennsylvania Law Review* 1034 (May 2007).

Notes to Chapter Eight

131 "Percentage of Americans with Stock Hits Eleven Year Low, Gallup Says," *Huffington Post* (April 21, 2011), www.huffingtonpost.com/2011/04/21/stock-market-us-real-estate-gallup_n_851786.html

132 Lynn Stout, *Cultivating Conscience: How Good Laws Make Good People* (Princeton and Oxford: Princeton University Press, 2011), 98.

133 Einer Elhauge, "Sacrificing Corporate Profits in the Public Interest," 80 *New York University Law Review* 793 (2005). A 2011 survey of individuals in the top quarter of wage-earners in different countries found that nearly half of those in the U.S. disagreed with Milton Friedman's proposition that the only social responsibility of business is to increase its profits. "Attitudes to Business: Milton Friedman Goes on Tour," *Economist* 63 (January 29, 2011).

134 See generally www.sristudies.org/Key+Studies.

135 The Forum for Sustainable and Responsible Investment estimates that one in every eight dollars under professional management in the U.S. is now in a socially responsible fund, http://ussif.org/resources/sriguide/srifacts.cfm.

136 Elhauge, "Sacrificing Corporate Profits," 733.

137 Id., 792.

138 Stout, *Cultivating Conscience,* 94.

139 Stout, *Cultivating Conscience,* 118.

140 Elhauge, "Sacrificing Corporate Profits," 800–801.

141 Joel Bakan, *The Corporation: The Pathological Pursuit of Profit and Power* (New York, London, Toronto, Sydney: Free Press, 2004), 37, 60.

[142] Ian B. Lee, "Corporate Law, Profit Maximization, and the 'Responsible' Shareholder," 10 *Stanford Journal of Law, Business and Finance* 71 (2005).

[143] Ivar Kolstad, "Why Firms Should Not Always Maximize Profits," Vol. 76, No. 2 *Journal of Business Ethics* 143–144 (2007); Forum for Sustainable and Responsible Investment, "Performance and Socially Responsible Investment, ussif.org /resources/performance.cfm.

Notes to the Conclusion

[144] *Louis K. Liggett Co. et al. v. Lee, Comptroller et al.*, 288 U.S. 517 (1933) 548, 567.

[145] Cynthia L. Estlund, "Working Together: The Workplace, Civil Society, and the Law," 89 *Georgetown Law Journal* 1, 3–5 (2000).

[146] Darrell West, *The Purpose of the Corporation in Business and Law School Curricula* (Brookings, July 19, 2011) www .brookings.edu/~/media/Files/rc/papers/2011/0719 _corporation_west/0719_corporation_west.pdf., 17–18

[147] Nassim Nicholas Taleb, *The Black Swan: The Impact of the Highly Improbable* (New York: Random House, 2007), 69.

[148] Michael C. Jensen, "Value Maximization, Stakeholder Theory, and the Corporate Objective Function," 12 *Business Ethics Quarterly* 238 (April, 2002).

[149] Id., 235.

[150] William T. Allen, "Our Schizophrenic Conception of the Business Corporation," 14 Cardozo Law Review 261, 280 (1992).

[151] Iman Anabtawi, "Some Skepticism About Increasing Shareholder Power," 53 *University of California Los Angeles Law Review* 561, 564 (2006).

[152] West, *The Purpose of the Corporation*, 3.

Index

About the Author

Lynn Stout is the Distinguished Professor of Corporate and Business Law, Clarke Business Law Institute, at Cornell Law School. She is the author of more than forty books and articles on corporate governance, financial regulation, law and economics, and moral behavior. She is an internationally recognized expert who lectures widely and has written for the *Wall Street Journal*, the *New York Times*, and the *Financial Times*.

Stout is deeply involved with and committed to the business world. She serves as an independent trustee and chair of the governance committee for the Eaton Vance family of mutual funds; as a member of the board of advisors for the Aspen Institute's Business & Society Program; as an executive advisor to the Brookings Institution's project on the purpose of the corporation; and as a research fellow for the Gruter Institute for Law and Behavioral Research. She has also served as principal investigator and founder of the UCLA-Sloan Foundation Research Program on Business Organizations; as a member of the American Bar Association's Task Force on the Changing Nature of Board/Shareholder Relations; as a member of the board of directors of the American Law and Economics Association; as chair of the American Association of Law Schools

Section on Law and Economics; and as chair of the American Association of Law Schools Section on Business Associations.

Stout believes that given the right laws, business in general and corporations in particular have enormous potential to do good in the world. Her most recent book is *Cultivating Conscience: How Good Laws Make Good People* (Princeton University Press, 2011).

Berrett–Koehler
Publishers

Berrett-Koehler is an independent publisher dedicated to an ambitious mission: *Creating a World That Works for All*.

We believe that to truly create a better world, action is needed at all levels—individual, organizational, and societal. At the individual level, our publications help people align their lives with their values and with their aspirations for a better world. At the organizational level, our publications promote progressive leadership and management practices, socially responsible approaches to business, and humane and effective organizations. At the societal level, our publications advance social and economic justice, shared prosperity, sustainability, and new solutions to national and global issues.

A major theme of our publications is "Opening Up New Space." Berrett-Koehler titles challenge conventional thinking, introduce new ideas, and foster positive change. Their common quest is changing the underlying beliefs, mindsets, institutions, and structures that keep generating the same cycles of problems, no matter who our leaders are or what improvement programs we adopt.

We strive to practice what we preach—to operate our publishing company in line with the ideas in our books. At the core of our approach is stewardship, which we define as a deep sense of responsibility to administer the company for the benefit of all of our "stakeholder" groups: authors, customers, employees, investors, service providers, and the communities and environment around us.

We are grateful to the thousands of readers, authors, and other friends of the company who consider themselves to be part of the "BK Community." We hope that you, too, will join us in our mission.

A BK Business Book

This book is part of our BK Business series. BK Business titles pioneer new and progressive leadership and management practices in all types of public, private, and nonprofit organizations. They promote socially responsible approaches to business, innovative organizational change methods, and more humane and effective organizations.

Berrett–Koehler
Publishers

A community dedicated to creating
a world that works for all

Visit Our Website: www.bkconnection.com

Read book excerpts, see author videos and Internet movies, read
our authors' blogs, join discussion groups, download book apps, find
out about the BK Affiliate Network, browse subject-area libraries of
books, get special discounts, and more!

Subscribe to Our Free E-Newsletter, the *BK Communiqué*

Be the first to hear about new publications, special discount offers,
exclusive articles, news about bestsellers, and more! Get on the list
for our free e-newsletter by going to www.bkconnection.com.

Get Quantity Discounts

Berrett-Koehler books are available at quantity discounts for orders
of ten or more copies. Please call us toll-free at (800) 929-2929 or
email us at bkp.orders@aidcvt.com.

Join the BK Community

BKcommunity.com is a virtual meeting place where people from
around the world can engage with kindred spirits to create a world
that works for all. BKcommunity.com members may create their own
profiles, blog, start and participate in forums and discussion groups,
post photos and videos, answer surveys, announce and register for
upcoming events, and chat with others online in real time. Please join
the conversation!